Angels
& Demons

We will destroy
your four pillars . . .

Angels & Demons

Foreword by
DAN BROWN

Introductions by
**RON HOWARD, BRIAN GRAZER,
& TODD HALLOWELL**

 NEWMARKET PRESS · NEW YORK

FIRST EDITION

10 9 8 7 6 5 4 3 2 1   10 9 8 7 6 5 4 3 2 1
ISBN: 978-1-55704-834-9 (hardcover)   ISBN: 978-1-55704-833-2 (paperback)

Library of Congress Catalog-in-Publication Data available upon request.

QUANTITY PURCHASES
Companies, professional groups, clubs, and other organizations may qualify for
special terms when ordering quantities of this title. For information, email sales
@newmarketpress.com or write to Special Sales, Newmarket Press, 18 East 48th
Street, New York, NY 10017; call (212) 832-3575 ext. 19 or 1-800-669-3903; FAX
(212) 832-3629. www.newmarketpress.com

Manufactured in the United States of America.

Special thanks to writer Linda Sunshine, designer Timothy Shaner at Night and
Day Design (nightanddaydesign.biz), and book project coordinator Seth Olson.

Produced by Newmarket Press: Esther Margolis, Publisher;
Frank DeMaio, Production Director; Keith Hollaman, Editorial Project Director;
Paul Sugarman, Digital Supervisor

Other Newmarket Pictorial Moviebooks and Newmarket Insider Film Books include:

The Art of Monsters vs Aliens
The Art of The Matrix★
The Art of X2★
The Art of X-Men: The Last Stand
Bram Stoker's Dracula: The Film and the Legend★
Chicago: The Movie and Lyrics★
Crouching Tiger, Hidden Dragon: A Portrait of the Ang Lee Film★
Dances with Wolves: The Illustrated Story of the Epic Film★
Dreamgirls : The Movie Musical
E.T. The Extra-Terrestrial: From Concept to Classic★
Gladiator: The Making of the Ridley Scott Epic Film
Good Night, and Good Luck: The Screenplay and History Behind the Landmark Movie★

Hotel Rwanda: Bringing the True Story of an African Hero to Film★
The Jaws Log
Memoirs of a Geisha: A Portrait of the Film
The Mummy: Tomb of the Dragon Emperor
The Namesake: A Portrait of the Film by Mira Nair
Ray: A Tribute to the Movie, the Music, and the Man★
Rescue Me: Uncensored
Rush Hour 1, 2, 3: Lights, Camera, Action!
Saving Private Ryan: The Men, The Mission, The Movie
Schindler's List: Images of the Steven Spielberg Film
Superbad: The Illustrated Moviebook★
Tim Burton's Corpse Bride: An Invitation to the Wedding

★Includes screenplay.

www.newmarketpress.com

Contents

Concept drawing of the Vatican Necropolis by production designer Allan Cameron.

Foreword

by Dan Brown

ROBERT LANGDON   DAN BROWN

Novelists are spoiled. I'm embarrassed to admit that I never realized this fact until I met filmmakers. Filmmaking, like novel writing, is about telling stories. This, however, is where any similarities end.

Writing a novel is a calm craft. It is embarked upon in solitude, often in one's pajamas before a crackling fire in the wee hours of the morning. Novels materialize at their own pace, often glacially slowly, and yet the novelist never checks his watch. He has no studio meetings, no conference calls with collaborators, and certainly no throngs of fans clamoring behind barricades to witness the magic of the process.

The novelist writes whenever he wishes and wherever he wishes, unfettered by the whims of anyone other than his own muse (whom he often simply ignores). He never worries whether his characters will arrive to work on time or whether they'll give a good performance. He is not bound by camera angles, expense accounts, or page limits. He bounces freely among points of view, mounts massive historical battles at no expense, and meanders off on tangents whenever the mood strikes him.

A novelist who wishes to set a scene inside the Louvre Museum need not negotiate with the French cultural minister. Nor must he gain the consent of the Italian police should he wish to send his protagonist on a car chase through

LEFT: Tom Hanks as Robert Langdon. ABOVE: Novelist Dan Brown on location during the filming in Rome.

11

A World Phenomenon

Albania

Brazil

Bulgaria

China

Czech Republic

Denmark

Estonia

Finland

France

Germany

Greece

Hungary

Iceland

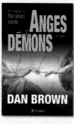
Italy

Japan

Latvia

Lithuania

Netherlands

Norway

Poland

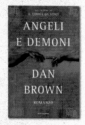

Portugal

Romania

Russia

Saudi Arabia

Slovakia

Slovenia

Spain

Spain (Catalan)

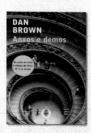
Spain (Galician)

Sweden

Taiwan

Turkey

United Kingdom

United States

Dan Brown sends his Robert Langdon character to such remarkable locales and puts him in such thought-provoking situations that I find him one of the most original and interesting heroes in popular literature. Dan's ability to create predicaments and dilemmas for Langdon that allow us to look behind the curtain and ask us to question long-held belief systems and perspectives on our contemporary world and our history is utterly original. And though his sprawling stories are challenging to adapt for film, both projects have been creatively gratifying and amazing life experiences. —RON HOWARD, DIRECTOR

Rome. A novelist never waits for the proper sunlight, or for traffic, or for a writing permit.

Don't get me wrong—writing novels is not easy.

That novels get written is impressive.

But that movies get made is miraculous.

Having now witnessed two of my novels brought to film, I must say that my respect for the challenges of filmmaking is exceeded only by my reverence for the brave souls who dare embark on such a perilous quest.

ABOVE: Director Ron Howard and novelist Dan Brown on location in Rome. OPPOSITE: Some of the more than 30 editions in print around the world.

With both *Angels & Demons* and *The Da Vinci Code*, I was privileged to watch some of moviemaking's noblest soldiers as they did daily battle and conquered Herculean forces. In Rome, they soothed the nerves of an anxious bride. In Los Angeles, they withstood the fury of an earthquake. And in London, they outfoxed the fox and filmed the impossible.

That movies get made is miraculous, indeed.

There are times when I think I, too, might like to try telling a story on film. For the time being, however, having watched the masters at work, I think I'll continue to fight my battles on safer ground . . . at home, in my pajamas, quietly typing before a crackling fire. ✠

Introduction

by Ron Howard

Throughout my directorial career, I've always been drawn to stories that feel fresh, a new adventure, both for audiences and for myself. And once I've explored that journey, lived with its characters, their individual dramas and joys, I'm eager to move on to the next discovery, a different tale, another world that will fascinate me, move me, and push me beyond the boundary of what I know.

That's probably why I've never made a sequel. Until now.

As a filmmaker it was clear to me that Dan Brown's *Angels & Demons*, a modern ticking-bomb thriller at the heart of a totally unorthodox mystery, would inspire a look and feel much different from *The Da Vinci Code*. That alone, while creatively enticing, was not the primary reason to make the film. In the end, it boiled down to Robert Langdon, as played by Tom Hanks.

I've collaborated with Tom on a comedy (*Splash*), a historical drama (*Apollo 13*), and now two mystery thrillers, and I have to admit that the scope and command of my friend's talent are an inspiration. In Robert Langdon, Tom has found a character who reflects his own intellect and fascination for the world. Both Hanks and Langdon are cool under pressure, practiced at letting their minds and imaginations lead them through intensely challenging moments. And like Robert Langdon, Hanks's sense of humor and personable nature should never be underestimated by any adversary. Tom not only relates to the character of Robert Langdon; he has a blast playing him and appreciates and respects (as do I) the particular way that these very original stories entertain.

These values resonated with me and our creative team as we were preparing to shoot the film. We went to Rome to scout locations and do research, blending in with all the other camera-wielding tourists, retracing Langdon's

RIGHT: Director Ron Howard standing on the top of the scaffolding at Piazza del Popolo while shooting on location in Rome.

Introduction

It was a little intimidating coming on the set because everyone had already worked together for many years and they were like bees in a hive. They work fast and they seem to have codes that they all understand. Also, I am the only woman among all these men. Ron kept telling me to relax. He wanted Vittoria to be strong, smart, and straightforward, but she is still emotional and feels responsible for everything that happened. —AYELET ZURER

For all of his making it look easy, or seeming not to take it too seriously, Ron is actually more fearless now as a filmmaker and takes much greater risks than he did when there was less at stake. It's not easy to make these types of movies; it requires this huge feat of engineering. You've got to go places and build things, but you also need a vision for how to bust open a genre so that it becomes personable and palatable. I think Ron is getting less slick as time goes by and he's making more complicated and dense movies at a time when other guys are turning it into a machine. Everyone on his team is pushing themselves even harder than they did just three years ago. —TOM HANKS

steps on the "Path of Illumination." On our way, it became clear that these churches—marvelous, truly awesome in their own right—were made even more so by what Dan Brown had brought to them: a sense of mystery and of historical insight. Inside these magnificent edifices, it's easy to believe that the rich and powerful move the gears of history invisible to most us, but that if we were only a little smarter, a little bolder, a little more focused, we could read the symbols they have left behind and understand our world a little bit better.

This symbol-reading, code-busting character that Dan Brown has created is no ordinary protagonist. With Professor Robert Langdon, Dan has built a hero for those of us who like their thrillers to be thought-provoking. Dan takes both the remarkable and the unremarkable from our everyday lives and events from our world's past, and weaves them into brilliant sets of clues to a mystery we never knew existed.

At the center of Dan's immensely entertaining novels are many real questions that define our lives, whether we think about them that way or not. In the case of *Angels & Demons*, questions are posed as to how science and religion coexist or why they are diametrically opposed.

And what better way to explore this schism than by showing one of the mysterious ways it has haunted us? In *Angels & Demons*, Dan resurrects the Illuminati, a very real group of enlightenment-age scientists, artists, and thinkers who warred with the Catholic Church over their different visions of the world and how it worked. Many contend that the Illuminati are still around today. I don't know if that's true, but anyone who reads the headlines understands that for all the progress the human race has achieved in the past 400 years, we are not so far from the same controversies the world faced in the time of Galileo. ✠

OPPOSITE: Ron Howard and Tom Hanks during a break on set. RIGHT: Associate producer Louisa Velis and director Ron Howard in Rome.

Introduction

by Brian Grazer

Ron and I discovered the world of Dan Brown in the same way everybody else did: we read *The Da Vinci Code*. Actually, we read it before it became a phenomenon, and it was like a magnet, pulling me into a world I didn't even know existed. When we finished the book, we both had the same reaction—we wanted to get our hands on anything and everything else Dan Brown had written, which led us directly to *Angels & Demons*.

Ron and I already knew that *The Da Vinci Code* was ripe material for a film, and *Angels & Demons*, if anything, was an even better candidate. In *Angels & Demons*, the Illuminati, a secret society that has long warred with the Vatican, resurfaces and kidnaps four Cardinals. With the fate of the Vatican at stake, Langdon races against the clock to follow the 400-year-old Path of Illumination and stop an unstoppable bomb. The Illuminati will murder one Cardinal each hour in secret locations all across the city of Rome—unless Langdon can follow the clues and stop them.

Sounds like a thriller to me. But what sets it apart, what makes it a cultural landmark, is what Dan Brown has brought to it.

Dan's genius as a novelist is in putting his finger on what makes us tick and building those ideas into page-turning thrillers. *The Da Vinci Code* was about the difference between belief and religion—that is, an individual's personal faith versus an organized codification of those beliefs. *Angels & Demons* has its own central question about the difference between science and religion: What can we prove, and what do we take on faith? It's no easy trick for those big ideas to become the driving force behind a plot that is, ultimately, a police procedural, but for Dan, it's second nature.

That is why Dan's books are a perfect match, if I may say so, for Ron Howard's excellence as a director: his great skill is in taking the big ideas of our time and putting them on a screen in an emotional, accessible, and moving

RIGHT: Tom Hanks and producer Brian Grazer.

18

way. Whether he is exploring the differences between the brain, intelligence, and the psyche, as in *A Beautiful Mind*, the ways one man can come to represent the hopes of an entire nation, as in *Cinderella Man*, or the ways that a life's dream can give way in an instant to a desperate hope for survival, as in *Apollo 13*, Ron can make an idea come alive on the screen.

I believe that Ron is the only director who could keep his foot on the accelerator, pushing the film forward at an ever-increasing pace, but also protecting the spine of the story, the thing people love about Dan Brown's books: those big questions.

As for me, I'm a fan of ideas, of interesting people who think. That's what makes Dan's books and Ron's films so intriguing to me, and I hope it's what will connect with audiences for *Angels & Demons* as well. ✠

ABOVE: (left to right) President of Imagine Entertainment Michael Rosenberg, 1st A.D. William Connor, producer Brian Grazer, and director Ron Howard. LEFT: Ewan McGregor as Camerlengo on the papal apartment set.

Preface

Re-creating Reality: From the Vatican to the Hollywood Park Racetrack

by Todd Hallowell

In making a movie like *Angels & Demons*, which is set in some of the best-known and beloved locations in and around Rome, one of our primary goals was to focus on re-creating reality. We wanted to make everything we built and shot look as real as possible, down to the most minute detail.

We were certainly under no illusion that we'd get any cooperation from the Vatican in filming *Angels & Demons* because the Vatican never allows anyone to shoot on their property. Besides that, *The Da Vinci Code* was not their favorite film for obvious reasons, so we did not anticipate any more favorable reaction to *Angels & Demons*, and knew they'd never make an exception for us. Giving them the opportunity to turn down our request would only create unnecessary controversy, so why bother asking?

Early in our preparation, though, we did want to get a firsthand look at the Vatican for our own reference. In many aspects, *Angels & Demons* is cinematically more challenging than *Da Vinci* in that it has huge action sequences and amazingly complicated sets, including the Vatican.

OPPOSITE: The real St. Peter's Square in Rome. BELOW: (left to right) 1st A.D. William Connor, director Ron Howard, producer Brian Grazer, and executive producer/2nd unit director Todd Hallowell.

On one of our first visits to Rome, we were given a fascinating tour of the Vatican that included areas like the headquarters of the Swiss Guard, where the general public is not usually allowed. At first, we were a little nervous when the Swiss guards recognized Ron but we soon realized that all they wanted was to have their pictures taken with him. Apparently, *Happy Days* is still wildly popular in Italy.

Our filming schedule included six weeks of exterior shots in Italy. We wanted to sprinkle the movie with actual location shots in and around Rome to give an overall feeling of authenticity. Once there, we kept a low profile and went about our business

Preface

PROGRESS 23JUNE08

in a quiet and diplomatic fashion, always conscious of the fact that we were working on their home turf.

We steered clear of shooting actual Catholic churches but were able to find locations that, when shot at a particular angle, would closely resemble the correct architecture. For example, we shot the exterior of a police station in Rome that had the same architectural feel as one of the church interiors we built as a set.

Once we completed our exterior shots in Italy, our plan was to move to London and shoot the rest of the movie on soundstages there. We had great success with this approach while making *The Da Vinci Code*.

We were just beginning to build our sets in London when we got a call from Sony, sometime right before Christmas of 2007. The studio asked if we could shoot our exteriors in Rome, as planned, and then bring the production back to Los Angeles. There were several

concerns factored into this request: the strength of the dollar against the euro and the ongoing writer's strike in L.A., among other issues.

It took about a month for the move back to L.A., and once we arrived, our sets, including the Sistine Chapel, were reassembled on the soundstages of Sony. In fact, for a long time over the summer months, we occupied almost every soundstage on the Sony lot.

ABOVE: St. Peter's Square set at Hollywood Park racetrack, 2008.
RIGHT: Director Ron Howard and executive producer/2nd unit director Todd Hallowell.

24

In addition to the soundstages, we also had to scout new locations for building our larger, outdoor sets. This was not an easy task, as the St. Peter's Square set, for example, was the size of two football fields.

Chris Baugh, our location manager, went on Google Earth and first located the Sony lot. From there, we started drawing concentric circles away from Sony to find a parcel of land that was both vacant and large enough to handle our sets. The nearest place we found was the Hollywood Park racetrack in Inglewood, which was only 8 miles from the studio.

We then began lengthy negotiations to lease 20 acres of their flat parking lot. Apparently, business was slow at the track and we were able to rent the space at a reasonable price.

So that is how we came to build St. Peter's Square on a racetrack parking lot in Los Angeles.

For several months, every time you'd fly in or out of LAX, especially at night, your plane would pass over an almost exact replica of St. Peter's Square. We heard that this was rather confusing to some passengers awakening from a long flight.

Allan Cameron did a staggering job re-creating Rome both at this location and on the soundstages. We knew that a large portion of our audience would be very familiar with these heavily visited tourist attractions, so we were under a strict mandate to get everything as accurate as possible. I feel confident that we succeeded in this task.

On all of Ron Howard's movies, including *Apollo 13*, accuracy and attention to detail have always been primary objectives. Ron often says that the real thing is going to inevitably be more interesting than the fantasy version. This proved once again to be true. When you actually dig in and do the research, what is revealed usually turns out to be more real and more entertaining than anything anyone could've imagined. ✠

Todd Hallowell has worked on fourteen films with Ron Howard and Brian Grazer, including The Da Vinci Code. *He is both the executive producer and the 2nd unit director for* Angels & Demons.

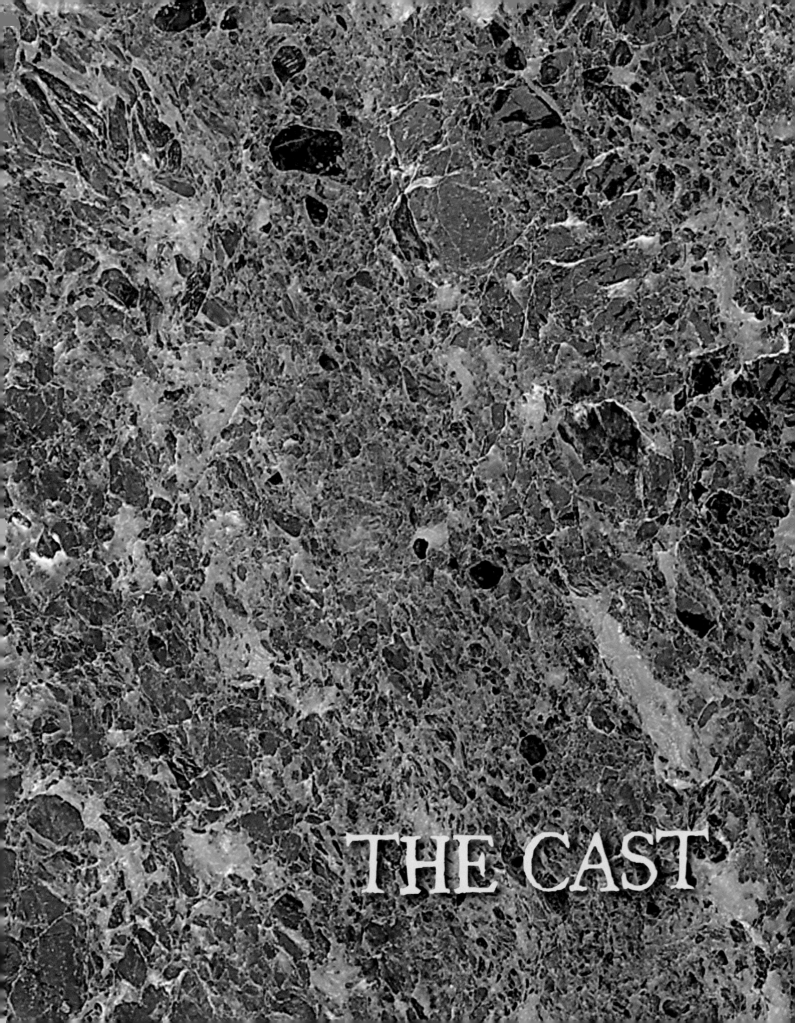

THE CAST

Tom Hanks as Robert Langdon

It's wonderful to play somebody who's smart. Langdon is an expert in this very obtuse field and is constantly collecting knowledge and then interpreting what it means. He's a symbologist; he studies symbols and is way ahead of anybody else when it comes to understanding all the permutations of what a symbol means and how it has meant different things throughout time. One symbol can represent five divergent points of view. Langdon is kind of like a massive crossword puzzle all the time. He's constantly living a game of *Jeopardy!*

—*Tom Hanks*

Tom Hanks's sense of the Langdon character along with his own intelligence, humor, and curiosity make him the perfect actor to bring this unlikely adventurer to life.

—*RON HOWARD, DIRECTOR*

ABOVE: The cast. RIGHT: Robert Langdon and Vittoria Vetra in a climactic scene in St. Peter's Square. OPPOSITE: Tom Hanks as Robert Langdon.

Ayelet Zurer as Vittoria Vetra

Vittoria is an Italian citizen. I decided that she grew up in Italy but lived in Geneva, which means she speaks French and understands German, which is quite similar to Italian, and of course English, which is the international language of science. Instead of her being an American with an Italian accent, I decided to make her international. I wanted people to understand what she's saying because the scientific stuff can be complicated.

Vittoria is an interesting character because she represents that generation of women who worked in professions that were mostly taken over by men. She's smart, strong-willed, and she doesn't take anything for granted.

The most complicated scene in the movie for me is where Vittoria tries to explain everything about the God particle and the canister. I studied hard for this scene and did a lot of research about particle physics.

—*Ayelet Zurer*

Ewan McGregor as Camerlengo Patrick McKenna

The Camerlengo is quite power-hungry and, like most power-hungry people, he believes in what he's doing. I always think it's more interesting to play somebody who's driven. No one really thinks he is a bad guy. Everybody has a reason for doing what they're doing. In Patrick's case, the reasons are extreme because he's an extremist. He believes that things should be changed, and he's capable of horrendous things to make it happen.

—*Ewan McGregor*

Richter is the head of the Swiss Guard, the security organization for the Vatican. He's in trouble, what with four kidnapped Cardinals and a bomb in the Vatican. But he's a pretty cool guy, so he tries to find ways to figure it out. He's a very controlled person and very religious. What we don't know is whether or not we can really trust him.

— *Stellan Skarsgård*

Stellan Skarsgård as Richter

I play Cardinal Strauss, and it's a very strong part. I've made 140 films and this was the best crew I've ever worked with. When I met Ron (Howard) for the first time, I had the feeling I'd known him for a very long time. He was very easygoing. Working on this movie was very exciting because everything was so authentic and original: the clothes, the sets, everything.

—*Armin Mueller-Stahl*

Armin Mueller-Stahl as Cardinal Strauss

THE JOURNEY BEGINS

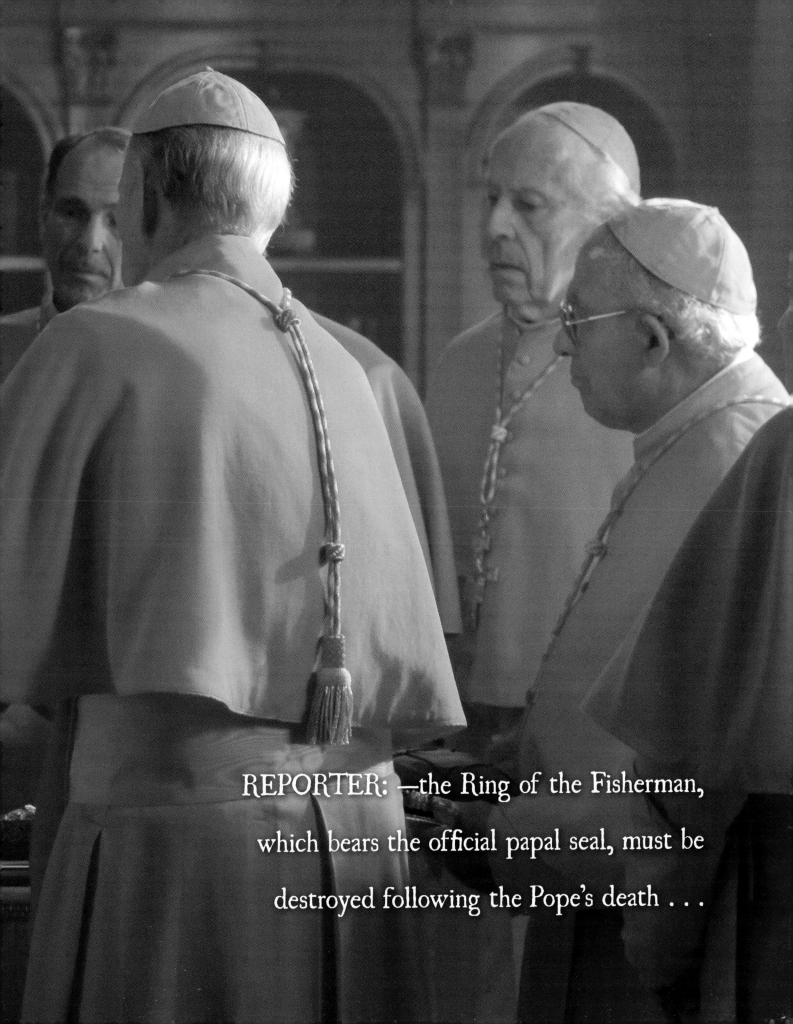

REPORTER: —the Ring of the Fisherman, which bears the official papal seal, must be destroyed following the Pope's death . . .

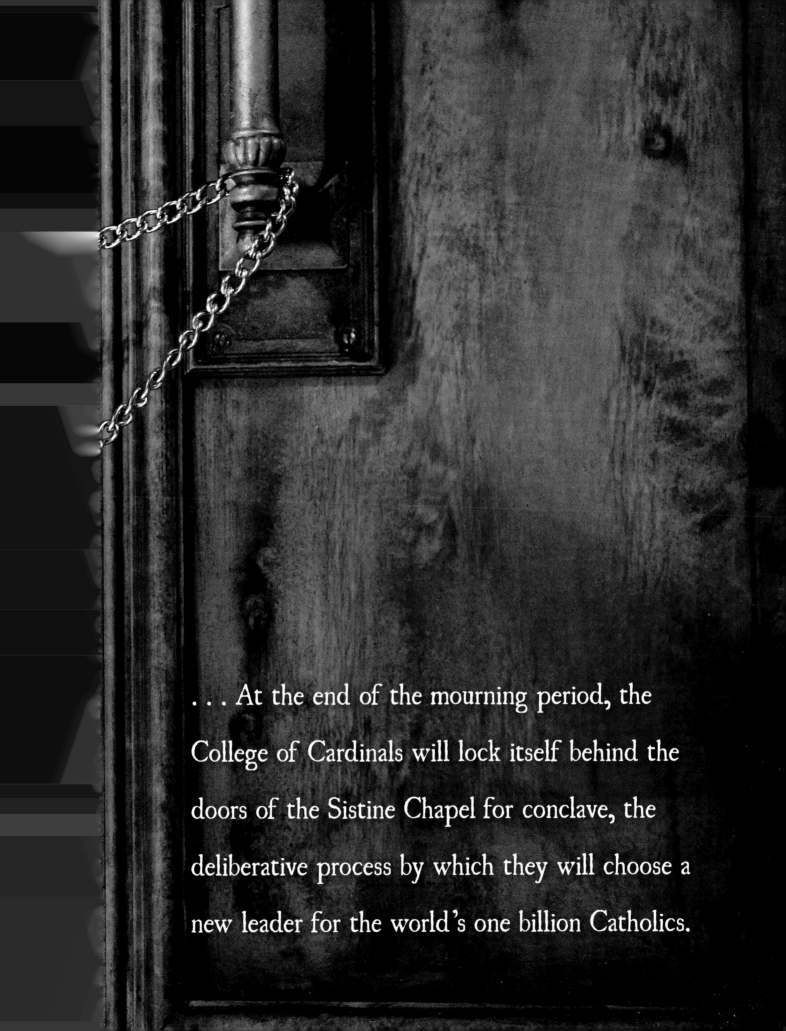

. . . At the end of the mourning period, the College of Cardinals will lock itself behind the doors of the Sistine Chapel for conclave, the deliberative process by which they will choose a new leader for the world's one billion Catholics.

The Sistine Chapel
Rome

One of the most popular tourist attractions in the world, the Sistine Chapel was built in the fourteenth century, commissioned by Pope Sixtus IV, for whom it was named. The wall frescoes were created by the greatest Renaissance artists of the time: Michelangelo, Raphael, Bernini, and Botticelli. Michelangelo's ceiling, 12,000 square feet that he painted between 1508 and 1512, is considered his crowning artistic achievement.

In addition to many other religious and papal functions, the Sistine Chapel is the site of the papal conclave, the ceremony for selecting a new Pope.

LEFT and ABOVE: The Sistine Chapel, Michelangelo's masterpiece, was recently cleaned during renovation. For the purposes of the movie, the paintings were re-created in the pre-renovated darkened palette to better showcase the actors and the action. BELOW: Portrait of Michelangelo by Daniele da Volterra, circa 1540s.

Michelangelo

Born on March 5, 1475, Michelangelo di Lodovico Buonarroti Simoni was an Italian Renaissance painter, sculptor, architect, poet, and engineer. His glorious sculptures *David* and *Pietà* were created while he was still in his twenties.

In 1508, even though he was best known as a sculptor, he was asked to paint the ceiling of the Sistine Chapel. His original assignment was to paint the twelve Apostles, but he asked for a more complex idea encompassing creation, the downfall of man, and the promise of salvation.

The final work took four years to complete and consists of more than 300 figures. Today, Michelangelo scenes from *Genesis* and *The Last Judgment* are considered among the most influential works in western art.

The Sistine Chapel Set

For the Sistine Chapel, we re-created everything accurately, from the mosaics on the floor to the paintings on the wall.

In Rome we began by having more than twenty people shoot the interior of the Sistine Chapel. We all took as many photographs as we could before we were told to stop. From

OPPOSITE: Shooting through Sala Regia, the anteroom for the Sistine Chapel, as it was re-created on a soundstage on the Sony lot in the summer of 2008. ABOVE: A scale model of the Sistine Chapel built during pre-production.

these images and others, we created a digital reference library.

Then my scenic artists did sketches, rather like what I presume the original artists did. We made mock-ups from those sketches, photographed them, and enlarged them to the correct size. These were then painted over. James Gemmill, the head scenic artist, did an amazing job.

I deliberately made the colors inside the Sistine Chapel just slightly more muted than they are today. The chapel was recently cleaned, which was quite controversial, but

I preferred it when it was slightly smoky and dark. I thought the costumes on the Cardinals would look better against that tonality.

The chapel itself was built full size on a Sony soundstage. The Sala Regia, which was the part of the chapel we used for the procession of the Cardinals, was scaled down slightly to fit on the stage.

It was quite a laborious, time-consuming effort that took between four and five months, but we got a very faithful reproduction.

—*Allan Cameron,*
production designer

SISTINE CHAPEL POSITIONS OF SCENIC IMAGERY
NORTH ELEVATION

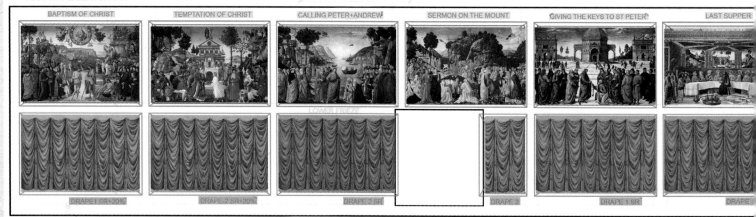

| BAPTISM OF CHRIST | TEMPTATION OF CHRIST | CALLING PETER+ANDREW | SERMON ON THE MOUNT | GIVING THE KEYS TO ST PETER | LAST SUPPER |

LOWER FRIEZE

| DRAPE1 SR+20% | DRAPE-2 SR+20% | DRAPE 2 SR | DRAPE 3 | DRAPE 1 SR | DRAPE |

THE LAST JUDGEMENT **SISTINE CHAPEL ALTARWALL**

ABOVE and LEFT: Murals for the Sistine Chapel. BELOW LEFT: The Cardinals walking into conclave. BELOW RIGHT: The Sistine Chapel under construction but almost completed, as seen in a photo composite.

SISTINE CHAPEL WIP—20 JUNE 08

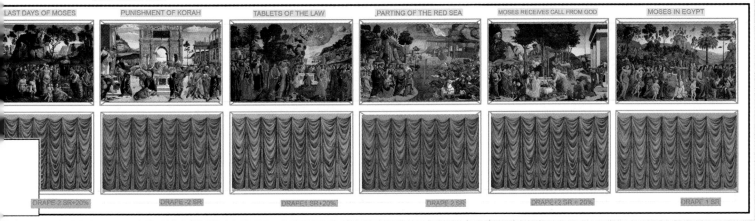

LAST DAYS OF MOSES	PUNISHMENT OF KORAH	TABLETS OF THE LAW	PARTING OF THE RED SEA	MOSES RECEIVES CALL FROM GOD	MOSES IN EGYPT
DRAPE 2 SR+20%	DRAPE 2 SR	DRAPE 1 SR+20%	DRAPE 2 SR	DRAPE 2 SR + 20%	DRAPE 1 SR

The Sistine Chapel, built to scale, was 40 feet high, which meant that 90 percent of the shots could be done for real. We built the famous ceiling as an artistic replica rather than duplicating the real thing. We deliberately introduced some differences in the creation so that we could say it is ours.

—*Angus Bickerton, visual effects supervisor*

Creating the Sistine Chapel during conclave was complicated, to say the least. Allan did an amazing job with all the wallpaper and everything else.

Our biggest challenge in terms of the props was to make the altar, the candlesticks, the crucifixes, and such. We could not just call a prop house or buy the stuff at Pottery Barn; we had to make everything.

We had carpenters building tables and carving these beautiful altars. We had an upholsterer and a sewing person pleating, sewing, and replicating the tapestries and such. The painters were marbleizing and painting.

Every set was a group effort from a lot of talented people who worked really hard. It really brought out the best in everyone.

—*Bob Gould, set decorator*

When I saw the actors and extras who were playing the Cardinals entering the Sistine Chapel set on the first day . . . the expressions on their faces mirrored the expressions that I'd seen on the faces all around me the handful of times I'd been in the Sistine Chapel before. I think, like me, they felt a particular pride as show people being involved with a movie-making situation as rarefied as this one.

—RON HOWARD, DIRECTOR

When it comes to art direction, you're in high country when you're re-creating the Sistine Chapel. You could say, look, we're going to pretend the College of Cardinals doesn't take place in the Sistine Chapel; it takes place in Glendale and looks kind of ornate. But there's no point in doing Angels & Demons if you're going to scrimp on that kind of version of it.

—TOM HANKS

The altar in the Sistine Chapel was re-created in amazing detail.

Sala Regia

The task of re-creating the paintings in the Sistine Chapel was the job of James Gemmill, a scenic artist who first worked with Allan Cameron on *The Mummy*. "The Sistine Chapel has a unique status as a symbol of all that is stunning and beautiful, and it was amazing to be asked to duplicate it," admits Gemmill.

Most of the paintings were made to actual size. First, the art department compiled numerous photos in various degrees of quality. "With these and my own sketches I was able to re-create to scale and to some degree the surfaces of the works of art," explains Gemmill. "The computer was used to enlarge some areas of detail, but all the images needed to be fully painted

and realized regardless of any use of mechanical devices."

Work began in London and continued in Los Angeles when the production moved back to the U.S. It took about five months to complete the task, and Gemmill was assisted by two fellow artists, Russell Oxley in England and Gunnar Ahmer in L.A.

Gemmill is convinced that, in many ways, the original artwork in the Sistine Chapel was produced in a manner similar to that for the film. "It was a commissioned work that not only required images, but was completed under time and budget constraints, and with some of the same artistic and labor issues we had," explains the artist. "I am also convinced that Michelangelo had a team of artists who painted a great many of the figures, as a head scenic

artist would. In 'The Last Judgment,' for example, I found artistic blunders that could only have been done by eyes and hands other than those of Michelangelo."

Despite the enormous task at hand, the greatest challenge for the artists was meeting their tight deadlines. That, and the weather. "The hardest part," Gemmill says, "was trying to keep warm while painting in England, and trying to stay cool while working in L.A."

ABOVE: The Sala Regia set. LEFT: Lead scenic artist James Gemmill working on the Michelangelo paintings. RIGHT: Director of photography Salvatore Totino on the Sala Regia set. OPPOSITE: Swiss Guard actors on the Sala Regia set. FOLLOWING PAGES: Filming the conclave scenes on the Sistine Chapel set.

CLASSES OPPOSITAE TURCARUM UNA CHRISTIANAE SOCIETATIS ALTERA
INTER PIUM PONT MAX PHILIPPUM REGEM VENETAM REMP
INITO IAM FOEDERE INGENTIBUS UTRIM Q ANIMIS CONCURRENT

Costumes

The costume designer did a wonderful job. He did a lot of research, everything was accurate—the shoes, the trousers, the ring. When you wear the red suit and the cape, you walk like a Cardinal and feel like a Cardinal. It's wonderful. —*Armin Mueller-Stahl*

The Cassock

Ewan McGregor's cassock was made by one of the best ecclesiastical tailors in Rome. To make him look more regal, we used a beautiful satin finished wool with a capelet and hand-embroidered buttons. We wanted to give him some authority because he's just a priest who has taken on this huge role at the Vatican, which normally would be a Bishop or a Cardinal. Ewan's cassock is quite fitted, giving him an imposing look.

Walking around Rome we observed that so many of the clergy have their own style; some are sloppy, some are neat, some are thin, some are fat.

There are many companies in Rome that make ecclesiastical garments and they were helpful in our research and manufacture, especially since we never told them the name of the film.

—*Daniel Orlandi, costume designer*

ABOVE: Ewan McGregor in his tailor-made cassock. RIGHT: Daniel Orlandi's sketch for the Camerlengo's cassock. OPPOSITE: (left to right) Gino Conforti, Armin Mueller-Stahl, and Rance Howard, father of Ron Howard, who plays a Cardinal in the film.

I've worn a cassock before. I did a three-part BBC adaptation of Stendhal's novel *The Red and the Black* when I was young. In the story I played Julian Sorel, who is training to be a priest, so I'm no stranger to the black cassock. However, this one was made by the Vatican tailor who makes cassocks for the priests. It is really beautiful and I find it's quite a powerful costume to wear. I think the Camerlengo has a lot of reverential, still power and that kind of holier than thou, slightly above everyone else feeling that comes from wearing the cassock as well. —*Ewan McGregor*

CERN

CERN, which stands for the Conseil Européen pour la Recherche Nucléaire, is the world's largest scientific research facility. Located in Geneva, Switzerland, CERN employs over 3,000 of the world's top scientists and houses an underground particle accelerator that is over 14 miles long and stretches all the way into France. In addition, CERN (much to Americans' surprise!) is the birthplace of the World Wide Web. CERN's most incredible claim to fame, however, is that they were the first to manufacture something called *antimatter*—the most volatile substance known to man.

Antimatter is the ultimate energy source. It releases energy with 100 percent efficiency (nuclear fission is 1.5 percent efficient). Antimatter is 100,000 times more powerful than rocket fuel. A single gram contains the energy of a 20-kiloton atomic bomb—the size of the bomb dropped on Hiroshima.

In addition to being highly explosive, antimatter is extremely unstable and ignites when it comes in contact with anything, even air. It can be stored only by suspending it in an electromagnetic field inside a vacuum canister. If the field fails and the antimatter falls, the result is a "perfect" matter/antimatter

conversion, which physicists aptly call "annihilation."

CERN is now regularly producing small quantities of antimatter in their research for future energy sources. Antimatter holds tremendous promise; it creates no pollution or radiation, and a single droplet could power New York City for a full day. With fossil fuels dwindling, the promise of harnessing antimatter could be an enormous leap for the future of this planet. Of course,

mastering antimatter technology brings with it a chilling dilemma. Will this powerful new technology save the world, or will it be used to create the most deadly weapon ever made?

—*Dan Brown, author*

ABOVE: Concept drawing of CERN by production designer Allan Cameron. OPPOSITE: Scale model of CERN set. OPPOSITE RIGHT: The final CERN set.

The Super Collider

Allan Cameron went to CERN and returned with lots of great photos. Our job was to fulfill his vision of CERN. The main focus for the set was the collider, of course, where they are making antimatter.

Parts of our collider are from salvage yards, old aircraft graveyards, or any place where we could find different shapes and sizes of pipes and wires and such. We didn't really build it so much as marry together all kinds of found objects. Anything we didn't use, we put on the shelves to look like they were in storage. So we had all this braided wire and these canisters as set dressing.

I'd love to tell you this was an original thing that we copied and spent $300,000 building, but really this was more like a scavenger hunt.

—Bob Gould, set decorator

ABOVE: Photoshop composite image used to pre-visualize a scene in CERN.
BELOW: The antimatter room on the film's CERN set. OPPOSITE PAGE:
Carmen Argenziano as Silvano Bentivoglio, CERN scientist.

We recently got the news that they have just started up the accelerator at CERN and it will take some time before they get up to speed. Years ago, Dan Brown was somehow ahead of the game when he was writing about this. Our timing is kind of perfect as far as making this movie goes. —Tom Hanks

Entanglement Science

In the last few years, scientists have found themselves face to face with facts that force them to rethink the world in which we live. Their discoveries have implications in not only the physical realm but the philosophical and spiritual as well. The heroine of *Angels & Demons* is actually one of these CERN scientists—a brilliant marine biologist who is a specialist in "Entanglement Science," the study of the interconnectivity of all things. Many of the marine experiments she runs in the novel are real-life experiments that have been run in the last few years. And, as anyone who's read *Angels & Demons* can attest, the results are unnerving. There are those who believe science will someday prove God exists. Either way, scientists are certainly starting to tackle some of life's most profound spiritual questions. Of course, these sacred questions have always been the domain of the clergy. And a new battle is raging over who will be providing answers to life's deepest mysteries. . . science or religion?

—*Dan Brown, author*

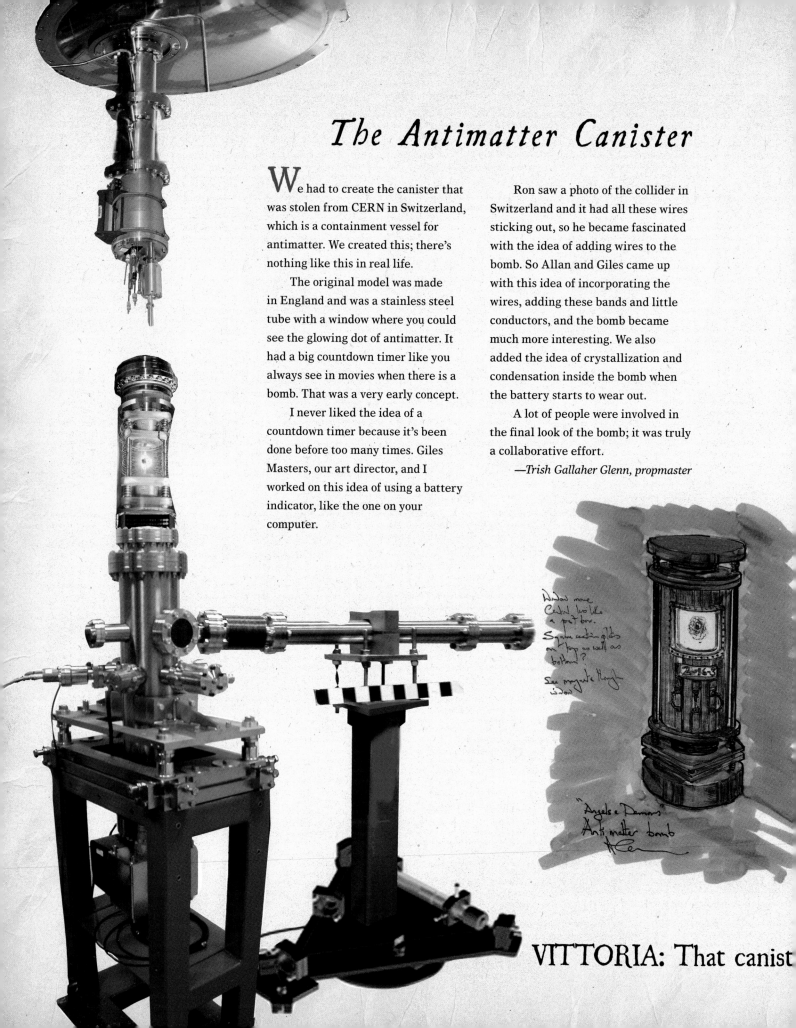

The Antimatter Canister

We had to create the canister that was stolen from CERN in Switzerland, which is a containment vessel for antimatter. We created this; there's nothing like this in real life.

The original model was made in England and was a stainless steel tube with a window where you could see the glowing dot of antimatter. It had a big countdown timer like you always see in movies when there is a bomb. That was a very early concept.

I never liked the idea of a countdown timer because it's been done before too many times. Giles Masters, our art director, and I worked on this idea of using a battery indicator, like the one on your computer.

Ron saw a photo of the collider in Switzerland and it had all these wires sticking out, so he became fascinated with the idea of adding wires to the bomb. So Allan and Giles came up with this idea of incorporating the wires, adding these bands and little conductors, and the bomb became much more interesting. We also added the idea of crystallization and condensation inside the bomb when the battery starts to wear out.

A lot of people were involved in the final look of the bomb; it was truly a collaborative effort.

—*Trish Gallaher Glenn, propmaster*

VITTORIA: That canist

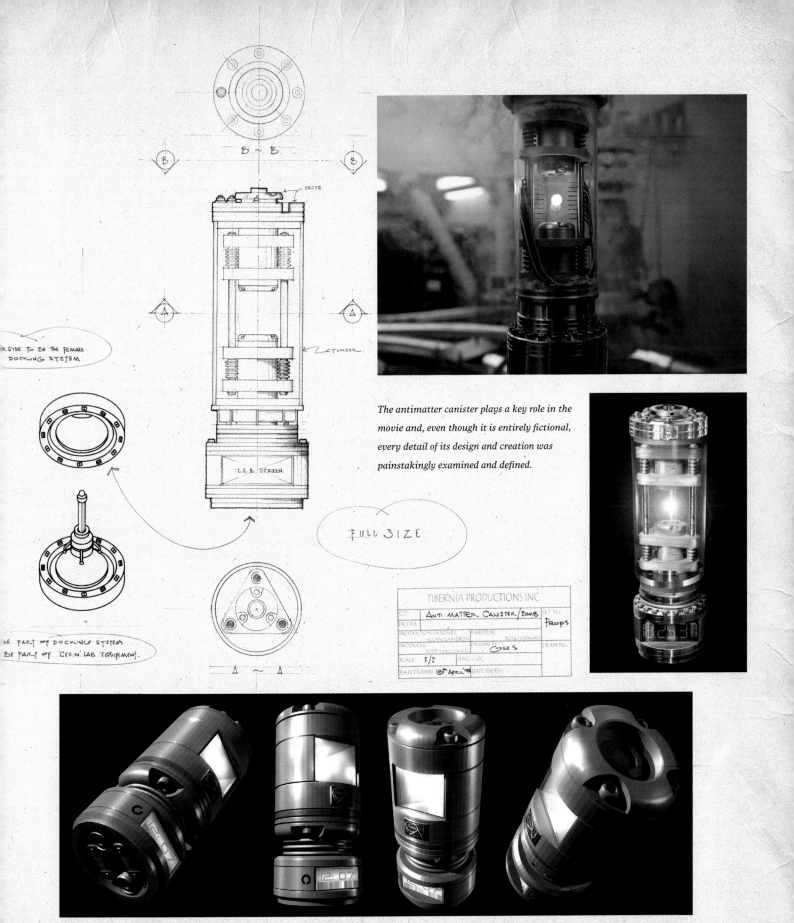

The antimatter canister plays a key role in the movie and, even though it is entirely fictional, every detail of its design and creation was painstakingly examined and defined.

B ~ B.

FULL SIZE

L.E.D. SCREEN.

SIDE TO BE THE FEMALE
DOCKING SYSTEM

PART OF DOCKING SYSTEM
BE PART OF 'CERN' LAB EQUIPEMENT.

TIBERNIA PRODUCTIONS INC.		
SET	ANTI MATTER CANISTER / BOMB	SET No.
DETAIL		PROPS
PRODUCTION DESIGNER ALLAN CAMERON	DIRECTOR RON HOWARD	
PRODUCER TODD HALLOWELL	DRAWN BY GILES	DRAW No.
SCALE F/S	STAGE / LOC	
DATE DRAWN 18ᵗʰ APRIL '08	DATE ISSUED	

ntains an extremely combustible substance called antimatter.

Langdon's Apartment

Langdon's apartment was an interesting set, as this is the first time since *The Da Vinci Code* that we get to see where he lives. Allan [Cameron] particularly wanted to show Langdon's personality in the way we dressed this set. We had input from passages in Dan Brown's book and from some of the studio executives.

We paid careful attention to the books on the shelves, the kind of mail on the desk, his swimming trophies, family photos, and his eclectic collection of artifacts from around the world. As always, Ron wanted us to also dress the inside of the drawers on Langdon's desk. This was a small set, but it showed a lot of character in the details. —*Cheryl Gould, lead person*

ABOVE and BELOW LEFT: All the details of Langdon's apartment were designed to showcase his interests and studies. BELOW RIGHT: (left to right) Tom Hanks, David Pasquesi, and Ron Howard during shooting.

Dressing the Symbologist

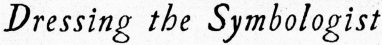

Tom Hanks is again playing Robert Langdon, Harvard symbologist. Our goal was to make it seem that he was really from Harvard. After looking at pictures of so many different Harvard professors, we discovered they all dress differently. We went to Dan Brown's book, which describes Langdon wearing a tweed jacket, and used that image as a starting point.

Tom basically wears one outfit through most of the movie, which makes it surprisingly hard for the costume department. We needed to consider all the things he has to do throughout the movie and how that affects his clothing. In this movie, Hanks breaks through windows and crawls around small, dirty spaces. He goes through water, fire, and blood, and not in any sequence in terms of shooting. Some of his scenes started shooting in Rome and ended in L.A. His clothes have to hold up and change through the course of the action.

We had to have seven different versions of the same outfit, one with a ripped knee, one with blood, a wet one and a dry one, a burned one, and so on. We did the burned one on the second day of shooting, and that used about a dozen jackets before we had hardly started. We also had about twelve versions of the jacket and twenty shirts for the stunt doubles.

It's a difficult process and involves a lot of testing, but none of this should be obvious to the audience, of course.

—Daniel Orlandi, costume designer

ABOVE LEFT: Robert Langdon, dressed in a custom-made Brioni suit, provided by the famous Italian clothier, with Vatican police officers. ABOVE: Daniel Orlandi's sketch for Langdon's tweed sportscoat.

Ambigrams

LANGDON: It's called an *ambigram,* the same backwards and forwards. That's common for a symbol, like a yin and yang, or a swastika, but this is a word. The Illuminati ambigrammatic symbol was considered a myth for four centuries. Supposedly a sixteenth-century artist created it as a tribute to Galileo's love of symmetry, and it would be revealed only when the Illuminati had amassed enough power to resurface and carry out their final goal.

Ambigrams can be very unnerving when you first see them, and almost everyone who sees the ambigram on the novel's cover invariably stands there for several minutes rotating the book over and over, perplexed.

—*Dan Brown, author*

LEFT: *One of Robert Langdon's books,* The Art of the Illuminati.

John Langdon

American graphic artist John Langdon is known for his work with ambigrams, which form the basis of his book, *Wordplay*. He began developing what would later be known as ambigrams in the early 1970s. "I was fascinated with the yin-yang symbol and with the tessellated illusions that Escher had created with birds and fish and buildings," says Langdon. "*Angels & Demons* suggests that ambigrams are an ancient art form, but they are actually quite modern."

Langdon met Dan Brown in the mid-1990s when Brown was a musician and asked him to create an ambigram for his forthcoming CD entitled *Angels & Demons*. A few years later, Brown requested several ambigrams to use in his novel of the same name. Langdon was later surprised to discover he was the namesake for the main character in Brown's book. "I didn't know what to make of it," admits Langdon. "It was, of course, an honor, but I never imagined the book would become so well known and, by virtue of the book, so would my work."

Langdon has created logos for a wide range of clients from Jefferson

Starship to the American Board of Internal Medicine. Today, he is a professor in the graphic design program at Drexel University in Philadelphia and continues to work on ambigrams, among many other creative pursuits.

ABOVE: Dan Brown (left) with John Langdon.

The Branding Irons

Allan Cameron designed the case that holds the branding irons. Originally there were some really tricky design elements, and it opened in all kinds of complicated ways. But Ron felt it should look like an ordinary case; it was something the secret society carried around in the streets and needed to look inconspicuous.

We gathered together a lot of vintage cases and took the details we liked best from various cases. We built this beautiful new leather case and aged it a little bit. Then we showed it to Ron and he said, "Gosh, I think it needs to look really beat up."

So, all of that night and the following morning, until we had to put it on camera, five pairs of hands were on this case—scratching with knives, screwdrivers, wire brushes, sandpaper, and other aging materials. Everybody did a little bit of aging, even Allan Cameron and Ron did a little gouging.

And this is what we wound up with.

—*Trish Gallaher Glenn, propmaster*

RIGHT: Concept illustration of the branding iron case designed by Allan Cameron.
ABOVE: The final prop used in the film.

VATICAN / SECURITY. OFFICE.

Richter's Desk with concealed monitor
Giles Masters 8th May 2008

When Vittoria's notebooks are removed the monitor will rotate to active mode.

Key activates sliding panel that reveals Vittoria's notebooks

Vatican City Security Room

The Vatican City security room almost looks like a bomb shelter, but it is a real armory with everything from primitive weapons to computers. We could only find four pieces of armor in Italy, which we rented for a week. We used these pieces to make our armor from molded plastic, which we painted to look like metal.

The guns are replicas we either purchased online or rented. Allan (Cameron) designed the sword racks, and those we made in our shop. Allan then made these great frescoes for the walls.

Allan's idea was that it should look practical. So we have this old beautiful building and then maybe a console from the 80s. They haven't just bought high-tech consoles; these look like they've been there for thirty years. —*Bob Gould, set decorator*

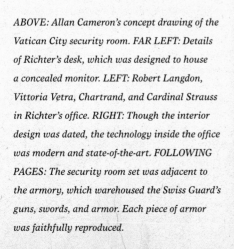

ABOVE: Allan Cameron's concept drawing of the Vatican City security room. FAR LEFT: Details of Richter's desk, which was designed to house a concealed monitor. LEFT: Robert Langdon, Vittoria Vetra, Chartrand, and Cardinal Strauss in Richter's office. RIGHT: Though the interior design was dated, the technology inside the office was modern and state-of-the-art. FOLLOWING PAGES: The security room set was adjacent to the armory, which warehoused the Swiss Guard's guns, swords, and armor. Each piece of armor was faithfully reproduced.

The Swiss Guard

Vatican City has been protected by the Swiss Guard since early in the fifteenth century. Pope Julius II granted them the title "Defenders of the Church's freedom."

Over the years, the Guard has both expanded and shrunk in size and was even disbanded. Today, the papal Swiss Guard have taken over the ceremonial roles of former units of guard. In 2005, there were 134 members of the Swiss Guard.

The official dress uniform is a colorful Renaissance design of blue, red, orange, and yellow. Members also wear a long sword.

LEFT and BELOW: Details showing the different offices and armory of the Swiss Guard.

Dressing
   the Guard

The official story is that the colorful Swiss Guard uniform was originally designed by Michelangelo.

To be a member of the Swiss Guard, you have to be Swiss, a devout Catholic, trained by the Swiss military, and, for the first three years at the Vatican, you must be celibate. So it's quite a commitment.

After extensive research, we made exact duplicates of their colorful uniforms and used winter-weight wool because it had a more interesting and rich feel.

—*Daniel Orlandi, costume designer*

ABOVE and RIGHT: The colorful uniforms of the Swiss Guard are thought to have been designed by Michelangelo, though that might just be a brilliant rumor. LEFT: Daniel Orlandi's sketch for the Swiss Guard costume.

Vatican Archive

The Vatican archives warehouse untold masterpieces of art but no one in the film company had seen the actual place; only one grainy photograph was available for reference. This left the creation of the set (this page) up to the imagination of production designer Allan Cameron. OPPOSITE TOP: The interior of the Biblioteca Angelica, used as a model for the film's library entrance that leads to the secretive Vatican archives. OPPOSITE BELOW: In all, more than 8,000 dummy books were created for the two scenes in the Vatican archives.

CAMERLENGO: Christianity

The Books

My biggest challenge in this movie, or ever in my life as a set decorator, was creating 4,000 books for the Vatican archive. I could not find that many old books in a store, and when I went to a bookbinder, they wanted a ridiculous amount of money. So I had them make 20 books and spent many long nights wondering how to reproduce them in such vast quantities.

I watched how they made the books at the binder by wrapping the cover around a block, so I copied that idea. I photocopied marble paper and then made a four-inch-thick cardboard box and wrapped the paper around it. I hired some kids to come in and make 4,000 of these boxes with the marble paper glued on.

These were for the books that were closest to the camera. For the additional books in the background, we used a vacu-form machine to mold out a whole shelf of books at one time. Then we painted those to look like old books. We also needed another 4,000 books for a different scene in the Galileo vault. These books were only two inches wide, so we had to make another huge set of dummy books.

The problem was the quantity and the volume of the books. You couldn't just paint a wall of books. We needed to show some depth so that the volumes looked real.

—*Bob Gould, set decorator*

ost sacred codices are in that archive.

LANGDON: This is
how Galileo got the word
out. The truth, not what
the Vatican forced him
to write. Smuggled out
of Rome and printed in
Holland on sedge papyrus.
That way, any scientists
caught with a copy could
simply drop it in water and
the booklet would dissolve.
Between its delicate nature
and the Vatican burnings,
it's possible this is the only
copy that remains.

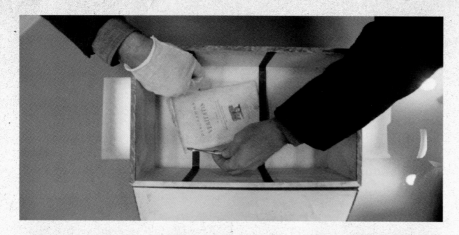

The Diagramma

We created the Galileo manuscript, called the Diagramma, for this movie. It's said that there's a real Diagramma in the Vatican archives, but none of us have been there, so we don't actually know.

We based the design of our Diagramma on other manuscripts from the era.

In Rome, I went to a collector who had some boxes that were from the Vatican from the late 1800s, and we used these for reference. We did a crazy amount of detail to age the box and the book.

The book itself contains a clue that is hidden in the gutter of the page. We did many, many tests to design the hidden clue in the illustration of the page. Ron was interested in having it within the border of the page, but we couldn't ever get it small enough or faint enough that you didn't notice it at one side or the other. So we got the idea of a watermark. We did tons of tests with companies that do real watermarks but, again, it was so small that you could never read it. So we created a tiny Illuminati symbol and had the actors use a magnifying glass.

—*Trish Gallaher Glenn, propmaster*

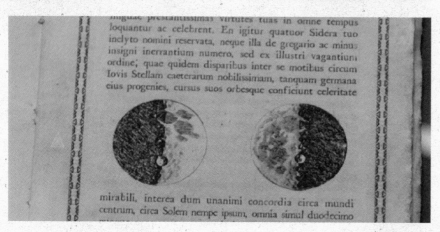

LEFT: Langdon and Vetra search the Diagramma for clues. OPPOSITE: Portrait of Galileo by Justus Sustermans, 1636.

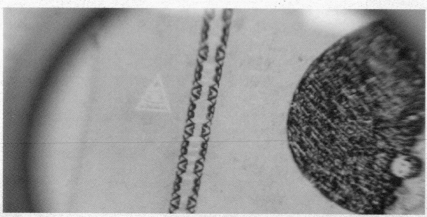

Galileo Galilei was born in 1564 in Pisa and was educated in the Camaldolese Monastery at Vallombrosa, south of Florence. Although he seriously considered becoming a priest, he entered medical school at the urging of his father. He soon chose to study mathematics and, in 1592, moved to the University of Padua, where he taught geometry, mechanics, and astronomy until 1610.

During this time, he made significant discoveries in many scientific fields. He was also interested in astrology, which at the time was seen as being related to other sciences.

A devout Roman Catholic, Galileo nonetheless fathered three children out of wedlock with Marina Gamba.

The Church denounced as heresy many of Galileo's teachings and observations about the planets.

Because of his book *Dialogue Concerning the Two Chief World Systems,* Galileo was placed under house arrest by the Pope and confined to his country house in Arcetri, outside Florence. He went blind in 1638, but continued to receive visitors until he died in 1642 at the age of seventy-seven.

Albert Einstein called Galileo the father of modern science.

The Illuminati

Secret societies like the Illuminati go to enormous lengths to remain covert. Although many classified intelligence reports have been written on the brotherhood, few have been published. Conspiracy theories on the Illuminati include infiltration of the British Parliament and U.S. Treasury, secret involvement with the Masons, affiliation with covert Satanic cults, a plan for a New World Order, and even the resurgence of their ancient pact to destroy Vatican City. Separating Illuminati fact from fiction can be difficult on account of the massive quantities of misinformation that has been generated about the brotherhood. Some theorists claim this plethora of misinformation is actually generated by the Illuminati themselves in an effort to discredit any factual information that may have surfaced. This concealment tactic, known as "data-sowing," is often employed by U.S. intelligence agencies.

It is historical fact that the Illuminati vowed vengeance against

the Vatican in the 1600s. The early Illuminati—those of Galileo's day—were expelled from Rome by the Vatican and hunted mercilessly. The Illuminati fled and went into hiding in Bavaria, where they began mixing with other refugee groups fleeing the Catholic purges: mystics, alchemists, scientists, occultists, Muslims, Jews. From this mixing pot, a new Illuminati emerged. A darker Illuminati. A deeply anti-Christian Illuminati. They grew very powerful, infiltrating power structures, employing mysterious rites, retaining deadly secrecy, and vowing someday to rise again and take revenge on the Catholic Church.

Angels & Demons is a thriller about the Illuminati's long-awaited resurgence and vengeance against their oppressors. . . but most of all, it is a story about Robert Langdon, the Harvard symbologist who gets caught in the middle.

—*Dan Brown, author*

Concept art developed in pre-production.

The Path of
Illumination

VITTORIA: Galileo was Illuminati?

LANGDON: And a devout Catholic. He thought science and religion weren't enemies, but two different languages telling the same story. He wanted like minds to be able to find the Church of Illumination, but he couldn't exactly advertise its location, so he created a coded path . . . Then, an unknown Illuminati master sculpted four statues, each a tribute to the four fundamental elements—earth, air, fire, water—and placed them throughout Rome. Each statue held a clue, pointing to the next. And at the end of the trail was the Church of Illumination. If you could find it . . . you were one of them.

From Santi's earthly tomb

with demon's hole . . .

THE FIRST PILLAR

faith

The Pantheon

Named as the Roman temple "all the Gods," the Pantheon is the best-preserved building of its age, perhaps in the entire world. It has stood in the center of Rome for nearly 2,000 years.

First constructed in 31 B.C. and rebuilt during Hadrian's reign in 125 A.D., the Pantheon has been used as a Catholic Church since the seventh century. The main architectural feature is an awe-inspiring domed interior. The height and diameter of the interior circle are both an astonishing 142 feet, or 43.3 meters.

The shrines surrounding the walls of the Pantheon range from the glorious tomb of Raphael to those of the kings of modern Italy.

In continuous use since it was first built, the Pantheon has always been a symbol of the city of Rome.

OPPOSITE: Interior of the Pantheon in Rome by Giovanni Paolo Pannini, 1735. ABOVE: The real Pantheon and Piazza della Rotonda. FOLLOWING PAGES: Concept illustration of the Pantheon interior by Allan Cameron.

Shooting outside the Pantheon was one of the most grueling, yet exhilarating experiences of my career. Italian authorities allowed us to film with the understanding that we would not disrupt the flow of crowds for more than 90 seconds at a time. I rehearsed the actors rigorously, and we set about making 60-some setups over the course of two days amidst the chaos of the tour groups, paparazzi, and accumulating gawkers. The sequences were carefully prepped, camera setups diagrammed, and staging rehearsed, and yet it felt like a two-minute football drill for two straight days. Setting up was never the problem so long as we didn't block traffic lanes. Every time there was a take, crowds had to be cleared to the background, our extras moved into place, cameras rolled, and actors set into action. As soon as I yelled cut, tour groups charged through the frame, Tom and Ayelet were whisked to the sidelines, and it was a normal, busy summer tourist day at the Pantheon. —RON HOWARD, DIRECTOR

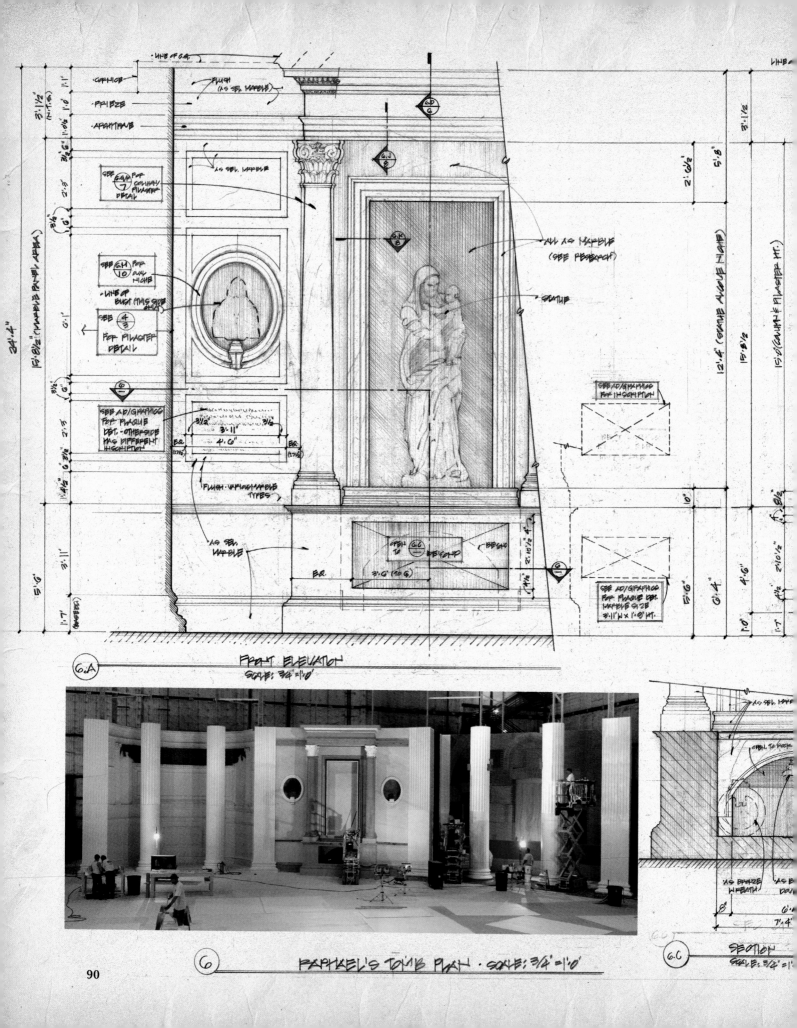

FRONT ELEVATION
SCALE: 3/4" = 1'-0'

6.A

90

6 RAPHEL'S TOMB PLAN · SCALE: 3/4"=1'0"

SECTION
SCALE: 3/4"=1'

6.C

Shooting the Pantheon

The Pantheon is an incredible building; a sphere 142 feet in diameter could fit inside. It is a real feat of engineering because they built this dome with a big oculus, a big hole, about 37 feet wide, in the center, through which rain pours in.

We built this set.

This is a symmetrical building with a number of chapels and aedicules (recesses) around it. Basically Allan [Cameron] built two aedicules and one famous chapel with the tomb of Raphael. This was built to scale on one of the Sony stages.

The chapel was built 30 feet high, and then the rest of it is a 3.5-sided green screen. Because it is symmetrical and the layout repeats, we were able to use it twice. Over the course of two days, we shot everything on one side and then we redressed it and pretended it was the other side of the church.

—Angus Bickerton,
visual effects supervisor

ABOVE: Visual effects supervisor Angus Bickerton on the set of the Pantheon while it was being dressed. LEFT: Scale model of the Pantheon. OPPOSITE: Some of the many architectural drawings for Raphael's Tomb. OPPOSITE INSET: Constructing the Pantheon on the Sony soundstage.

91

The Pantheon set showing the green screen area. During production, the filmmakers decided which parts of the set they would build and which parts would be computer-generated during post-production.

After the visual effects department finishes its work, the green screen area is filled in with computer-generated background imagery.

Raphael's Tomb

The statue above the tomb of the artist Raphael is called *Madonna del Sasso* (Madonna of the Rock), and was named because she rests one foot on a boulder. The work was commissioned by Raphael and made by Lorenzetto in 1524. The bust of Raphael is by Giuseppe Fabris and was created in 1833.

ABOVE: The tomb of King Umberto I. BELOW: Raphael's tomb, resting below the Madonna del Sasso *statue. RIGHT: The final set, a faithful reproduction of the original.*

VITTORIA: Raphael's tomb! But it's the wrong one... He was move

re in 1759. A century *after* Diagramma was published!

BASILICA

SANTA MARIA AD MARTYRES

LUOGO SACRO

MANTENERE IL SILENZIO

SACRED PLACE

SILENCE PLEASE

PANTHEON

Santa Maria del Popolo

Santa Maria del Popolo is the first church in the movie. To save money and to stay within our budget requirements, I used the same set twice.

In the script, the church in the Piazza del Popolo is under construction. So, for the exterior, we shot the police station opposite the church in Rome. We put up scaffolding to disguise the fact that it is not the church. Back on the soundstage at Sony, I built it as a church under construction.

The scaffolding gave me the opportunity to disguise the interior. Underneath the cloths and scaffolding is the set for another church, Santa Maria della Vittoria.

—*Allan Cameron, production designer*

ABOVE: Tracing paper covered the photograph of the exterior of the location, and Allan Cameron sketched the scaffolding that would be added to create the effect of the church under renovation. RIGHT: Photoshop images of scaffolding were added to photos of the real Popolo church. OPPOSITE ABOVE: A scale model of the church with the scaffolding in place. OPPOSITE BELOW: Vittoria Vetra, Robert Langdon, and Claudio Vincenzo in the Popolo church.

E̲ach of these set pieces called for a totally different approach, and they were inspired by films that we studied, sequences that we analyzed. Popolo was basically a haunted house sequence—very much about the fear of what's around the corner, what unseen villain is lurking, spying on our heroes, and what unexpected horror awaits them. —RON HOWARD, DIRECTOR

God Is in the Details

The church set for Santa Maria del Popolo, which was under construction, was covered with scaffolding and cloths. A great deal of thought went into the smallest details of dressing this set. "We had bags of cement shipped in from Italy," says Cheryl Gould, who helped dress the set. "In Italy, they use different construction lights and materials. Their tools are more primitive, as they still do things the way it's been done for centuries. Of course, their signage is unique from ours. We had to get all of those details correct, so we shipped a lot of things from Rome."

LEFT: Details from the Popolo church renovation, where even the cement bags were imported from Italy for authenticity. ABOVE: The Memento Mori statue re-created to the specifications of the original found in Santa Maria del Popolo.

101

LANGDON: It's the Chigi Chapel, in the church of Santa Mar

It was calle

The Chigi Chapel

One of six chapels in the Church of Santa Maria del Popolo, the Chigi Chapel was designed by Raphael and, more than a century after his death, completed by Bernini in 1520.

Fabio Chigi was Bernini's patron and became Pope Alexander in 1655.

Bernini's statue, *Habbakuk and the Angel,* celebrates the angel who took Habbakuk by the hair and transported him to Babylon to help Daniel, who is represented in the chapel on the opposite wall.

In the movie, the Habbakuk statue is one of the clues that helps to point Langdon to the Castel Sant'Angelo.

OPPOSITE: Vittoria Vetra, Olivetti, Claudio Vincenzo, and Robert Langdon entering the Chigi Chapel. ABOVE: The dressed set for the Chigi Chapel. BELOW: Scale model and architectural plan for the chapel. LEFT: The actual chapel in Rome.

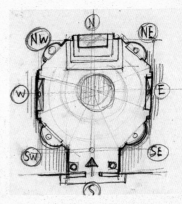

el Popolo.

apella della Terra, the Chapel of the Earth. Earth, the first element.

*W*hen we were on one of our early location scouts looking for statues we could shoot in Popolo, it suddenly popped into my mind that it'd be great if we could find a statue that embodied both good and evil in some way. And Allan Cameron kind of shrugged his shoulders and said, "Well, I suppose we could make that," and ultimately designed this half-angel, half-demon statue. —RON HOWARD, DIRECTOR

ABOVE: Concept drawing for the Angel/Demon statue in the style of Bernini. ABOVE RIGHT: Final hand-sculpted version of the Angel/Demon used in the film. RIGHT: Bernini's Habbakuk and the Angel *re-created for the film. BELOW: Self-portrait of Gian Bernini, date unknown.*

Bernini

Gian Lorenzo Bernini was born in 1598 in Naples, Italy, the son of a sculptor. At the age of seven, he went to Rome with his father, where his artistic talents were soon noticed. He became an apprentice to the painter Carracci and rose to prominence as a sculptor with several busts, including one of Pope Paul V, which he created when he was only twenty-two.

Bernini is frequently credited with creating baroque art and, throughout his life, remained its greatest exponent. His numerous works are scattered throughout Rome in churches, palaces, city squares, and local architecture. In April 1665, when he was at the height of his fame, he traveled to Paris, where the streets were filled with his admirers.

Bernini died in Rome in 1680, at the age of eighty-two, and was buried at the Basilica di Santa Maria Maggiore.

LANGDON: The unknown Illuminati master was Bernini.

Down the Demon Hole

ABOVE: *Pre-production reference photo of the original demon hole in Chigi Chapel.* LEFT: *Close-up detail of the first demon hole that Robert Langdon will descend into.* RIGHT: *The prosthetic body of the Cardinal that Langdon finds in the demon hole with the ambigram for "earth" branded into his chest.*

'Cross Rome the mystic

elements unfold.

THE SECOND ⬩ PILLAR

St. Peter's Square

St. Peter's Square represents the center of the Roman Catholic faith and, as such, draws pilgrims from all over the world. The Square is almost always crowded with people, especially during conclave, which is when most of the action in *Angels & Demons* takes place.

Because it was impossible to shoot at the actual location, the filmmakers had to create a very close facsimile. Thus, a massive set the size of two football fields was built on 20 acres in the parking lot of the Hollywood Park racetrack.

It would have cost many millions to re-create St. Peter's to size, so the set was scaled down to be about two-thirds actual size. "We had to save money," admits Allan Cameron, "but Ron wanted us to use as much real scenery as possible within the limitations of the budget. I spent a lot of time with the visual effects department and Angus Bickerton. We spent days and days and days talking about models, drawings, what we should build and what we should add by computer. We came up with a pretty efficient combination from a cost and a practical point of view."

Construction of the St. Peter's Square set began in the U.K. "Our set was designed for that location," says Cameron, "and then we moved to Los Angeles. The new site was more spacious, so we modified the designs. We shipped everything to L.A. It's difficult to ascertain how long the whole thing took because it was spread out over two continents, but I'd guess it was about five months all together."

Everything built was very faithful to St. Peter's Square in Rome, including the Bernini colonnades. Enormous 60-foot green screens were installed within the set so that additional people for the crowd scenes could be added, as well as the obelisk and the dome of St. Peter's, a spectacular cupola that soars high into the sky view.

LEFT: St. Peter's Square is almost always crowded with people. ABOVE: Detail of the "air" clue discovered in St. Peter's Square. FOLLOWING PAGES: Concept art developed in pre-production.

LANGDON: "West Ponente."
The West Wind. An angel blowing out five streaks of air. This is it!

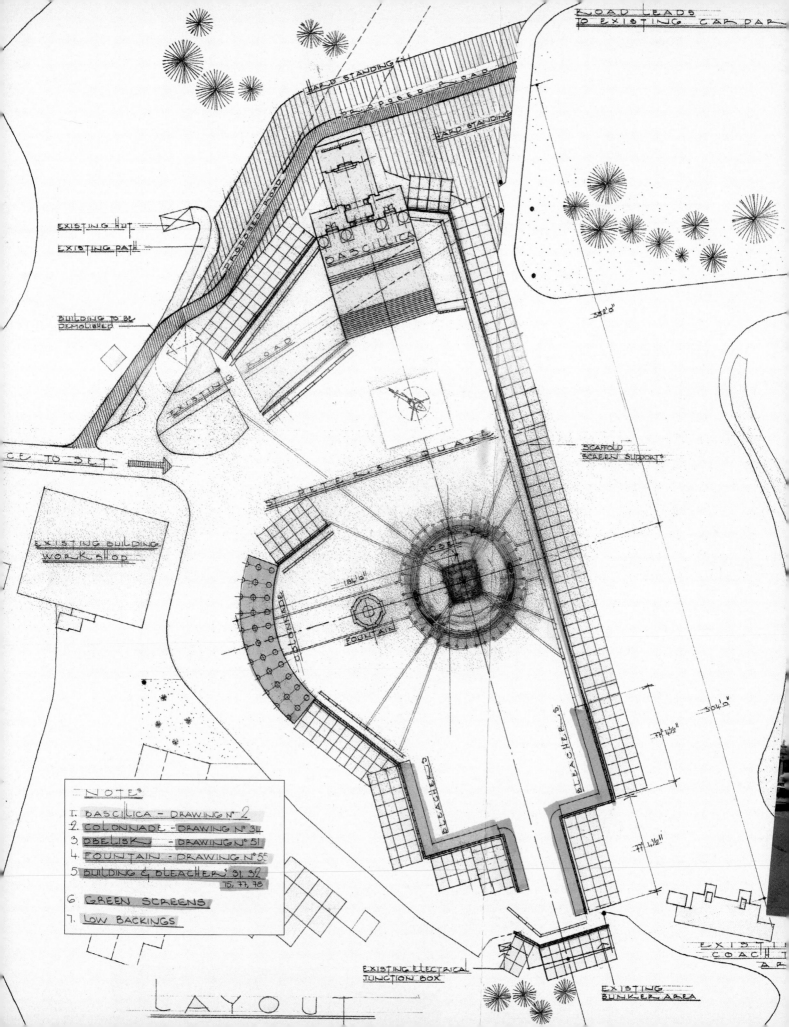

ROAD LEADS TO EXISTING CAR PARK

YARD STANDING

PROPOSED ROAD

YARD STANDING

EXISTING HUT

EXISTING PATH

BUILDING TO BE DEMOLISHED

BASCILLICA

PROPOSED ROAD

EXISTING ROAD

332'0"

SCAFFOLD SCREEN SUPPORTS

CO TO SET

ST PETER'S SQUARE

EXISTING BUILDING WORKSHOP

304'0"

184'6"

COLONNADE

OBELISK

FOUNTAIN

77' 4½"

BLEACHERS

BLEACHERS

77' 4½"

NOTES
1. BASCILLICA - DRAWING N° 2
2. COLONNADE - DRAWING N° 34
3. OBELISK - DRAWING N° 51
4. FOUNTAIN - DRAWING N° 55
5. BUILDING & BLEACHERS 31, 32
   15, 77, 78
6. GREEN SCREENS
7. LOW BACKINGS

EXISTING ELECTRICAL JUNCTION BOX

EXISTING COACH PARK

EXISTING BUNKER AREA

LAYOUT

Shooting St. Peter's Square

There are two fountains in St. Peter's Square; they are on opposite sides of the obelisk, which is in the center. In pre-production, we decided that if we built it actual size, it would've doubled or tripled the construction cost.

The colonnade was actually just under 60 percent of its actual size, but visually it looked larger. On our set, the gap between the fountain and the colonnade was seriously truncated, but if you were at eye level amongst the crowd, this perspective trick worked beautifully. However, that conceit falls apart when the camera rises up because then you can see that the distances are squeezed.

We knew that 85 percent of our shots would be done on ground level. So basically we built two models. If we were down at eye height, we would extend the set at the scale it was, because it worked as a visual trick. If we went up higher than 10 feet, we'd build a CG set that was actual scale.

—*Angus Bickerton, visual effects supervisor*

OPPOSITE: Technical plans for the St. Peter's Square set at Hollywood Park racetrack. BELOW: Location scouting montage of St. Peter's Square. ABOVE and RIGHT: Scale models for the St. Peter's set.

THESE PAGES and the FOLLOWING SPREAD: The parking lot of the Hollywood Park racetrack was the location for the St. Peter's Square set. These images show the progress of the set construction. After filming was completed for the St. Peter's Square scenes, the entire set was converted into Piazza Navona.

This is one of those films where I think we used just about every soundstage on the Sony lot. These are monolithic spaces; they are legendary and very specific. In re-creating these places, you can't scrimp on St. Peter's Basilica or St. Peter's Square. If you can't shoot in the actual place because of the tourists or the lighting or the permits, well, that's okay. Instead, we can build those places on a grand scale. —*Tom Hanks*

Faces in the Crowd

In St. Peter's Square, we're populating the crowd with between 200,000 and 400,000 people. Even in such a crowd, the striking thing is that, as a member of the crowd, you can only see the 30 or so people around you. You have to really get up above the crowd to see just how many people are in there.

Since the whole premise of the film is that it is taking place during conclave, and hundreds of thousands of the faithful are filling the square, that crowd is going to be blocking all of the views. We determined the maximum amount we needed on the shoot for a crowd scene was between 300 and 500 people.

After that, we have two ways to populate the crowd. One is that we shoot individual people on green screen and then duplicate them. We call those sprites. It's a painstaking process, but we have literally shot them in various ways: waving flags, being quiet, cheering, and then we shot them doing the same thing at 45 degrees, at 90 degrees, and then 130, so we basically have got this library of cards. Then we cut them out of the green screen and you put them on a card and then you generate 100,000 cards.

Our basic rule is that we need 40 to 45 different characters to not see repetition on the screen.

On top of that, we still wanted the option to do a computer-generated crowd, so we also brought a cyber scanner to the set. Again we take about 40 different characters—two nuns, two priests, two policemen, etc.—and make a full body scan of each one. We scan them in a relaxed position, arms slightly out from the body, until we have four 3D turntables of these figures. Then we go into a motion capture studio and we come up with a library of generic actions. For some of the really high wide shots, looking out over the whole of St. Peter's Square we have people milling, taking photographs, chatting with each other, praying, kneeling; we've got them doing bits of everything, really.

—*Angus Bickerton, visual effects supervisor*

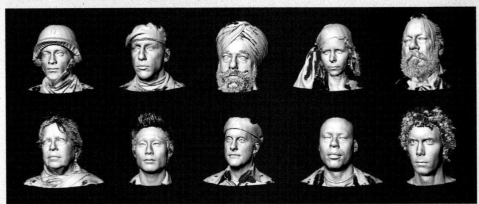

ABOVE LEFT: *The scenes at St. Peter's Square required a huge crowd of people. To shoot these scenes, hundreds of extras were filmed.* ABOVE RIGHT: *Thousands more people were added by computer in post-production.* RIGHT *and* BELOW: *Examples of cyber-scanned heads and bodies used to populate the crowd scenes.*

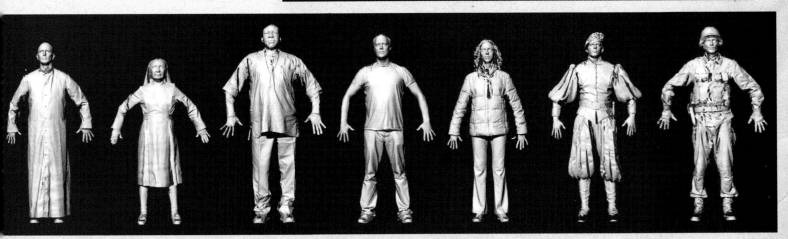

Dressing the Extras

For the crowd scene in St. Peter's, we dressed about 75 percent of the people. We had to re-create the Pope's funeral, conclave, and the crowds waiting for the announcement of the new Pope. For the funeral alone, we had 185 Cardinals in funeral garb, pallbearers, the Swiss Guard, priests, nuns, monks, Vatican gendarmes, bishops, patriarchs from the eastern orthodox religions, and all of the dignitaries who attended the funeral. Every single one of those extras had to be dressed, and so we needed about two thousand outfits just for that sequence. We also needed about two hundred Caribineri uniforms for various scenes throughout the film.

—*Daniel Orlandi, costume designer*

ABOVE: Daniel Orlandi's sketch of the funeral cape worn by Cardinal Strauss. RIGHT: Filming the funeral procession of the deceased Pope.

Inside St. Peter's Basilica

We obviously go inside St. Peter's Basilica, the church itself, which is amongst the top three or four biggest churches in the world. It is enormous. Cavernous. It is something you don't really appreciate until you go there, and no partial set could ever get close to replicating it. The dimensions just kill you.

Sony has some huge stages, 80 feet tall, but that's only half the height of St. Peter's. So Allan and I looked at that and asked, "What can we practically build?"

You can't cheat the scale that much.

We ended up building a very detailed confessio, a recessed area in the middle of the church, underneath the baldacchino, an enormous four-poster, ornate brass sculpture by Bernini that stands in the very middle of St. Peter's. The confessio leads down to the crypts.

Allan built a really fine replica.

Then we built as much floor as we could on Stage 14, and a hint of the bottom of one of the columns, with the famous sculpture of St. Peter. And that was it. Everything else after that was a 360 green screen, entirely a CG environment.

—*Angus Bickerton, visual effects supervisor*

ABOVE: The real St. Peter's Basilica in all its magnificent detail.

124

The sets for St. Peter's Basilica were done on the grand scale of *Gone with the Wind* or *The Wizard of Oz*. It ends up being a magical type of stage to walk into and perform in because the artists and craftsmen have re-created the space down to the finest detail. It ends up being the coolest thing in the world.

—*Tom Hanks*

RIGHT: Scale model of the Basilica's confessio. BELOW: The scene was shot with green screens, and the details of the Basilica were added in post-production.

Background details of the interior of St. Peter's Basilica were added in post-production. *ABOVE: The St. Peter's Basilica set with green screen. OPPOSITE ABOVE: The combined wire frame and grayscale CG model of the interior of St. Peter's Basilica, prior to the addition of textures and lighting. OPPOSITE BELOW: The final frame.*

Making Marble

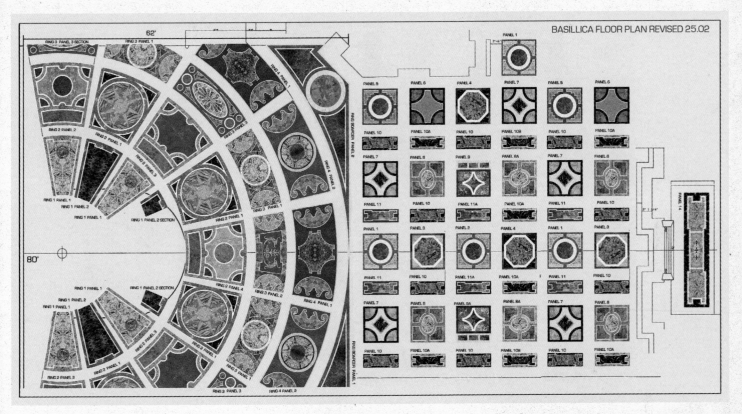

Many of the churches replicated in *Angels & Demons* have marble floors or wall panels with intricate designs. When it came to creating these sets, production designer Allan Cameron took photographs of 60 or 70 different pieces of marble at a London marble company. After creating a library of patterns in the computer, Cameron designed more than 500 different panels, which were then printed on paper.

These papers were hung on the walls and the floors of the sets. "By glazing the papers with different glazes and then burnishing them, we could create the look of real marble," explains Cameron.

This was time-consuming work, but in the end, the sets were amazingly vivid and realistic but somewhat delicate. To preserve the floors during shooting, everyone was required to wear paper booties over their shoes.

Creating the marble patterns of the churches in Angels & Demons *was a complicated task. Printed on paper and aged with different glazes, the paper looked permanent but was actually quite delicate and required that everyone on set wear protective paper booties, including director Ron Howard.*

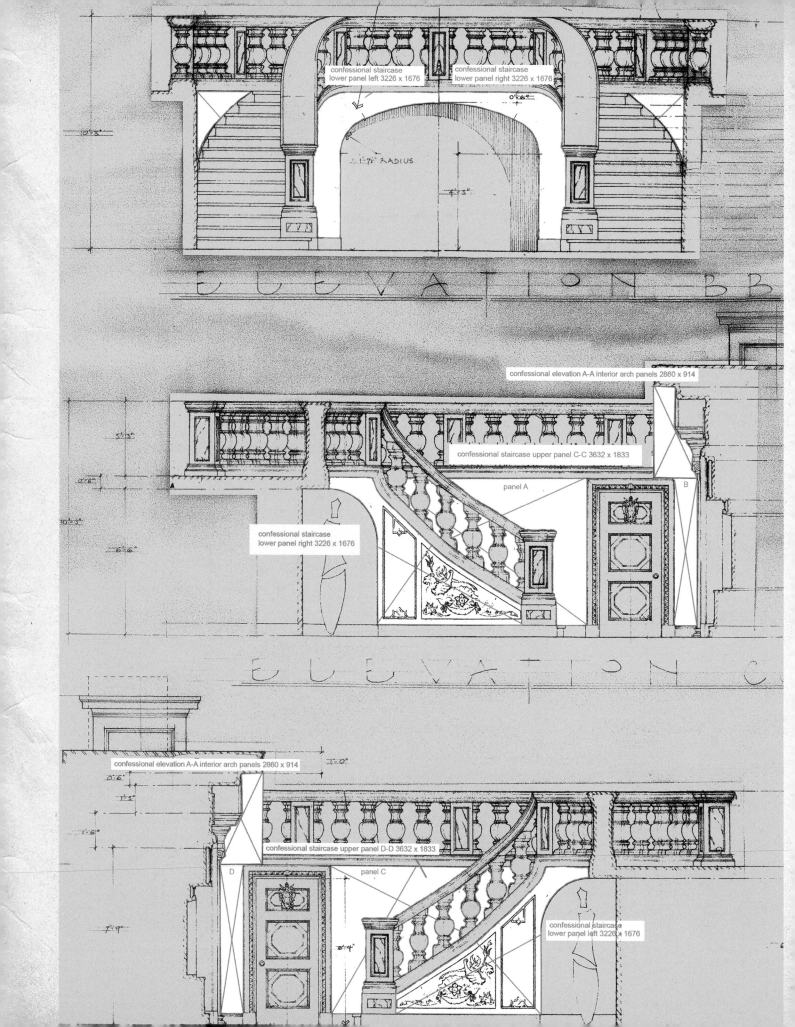

confessional staircase
lower panel left 3226 x 1676

confessional staircase
lower panel right 3226 x 1676

1'-7" RADIUS

E L E V A T I O N   B B

confessional elevation A-A interior arch panels 2860 x 914

confessional staircase upper panel C-C 3632 x 1833

panel A

confessional staircase
lower panel right 3226 x 1676

E L E V A T I O N   C

confessional elevation A-A interior arch panels 2860 x 914

confessional staircase upper panel D-D 3632 x 1833

panel C

confessional staircase
lower panel left 3226 x 1676

OPPOSITE: *Architectural drawings of the confessional staircases for St. Peter's Basilica.* ABOVE and RIGHT: *The finished sets looked remarkably real due to the attention to detail that was paid to every aspect of the set including the lights, alcoves, and plaques.* BELOW: *The real confessional staircases in St. Peter's Basilica, Rome.*

The Bernini Ledger

Artist Andrea Dopaso used watercolors to create the Bernini ledger, an important prop in the movie.

Following the execution of the "earth" and the "air" Cardinals, Robert Langdon (Hanks) rifles through an ancient ledger in the Vatican archives, looking for an important clue, the location where the "fire" Cardinal will be found. This prop, one of the most important in the film, was entirely hand-crafted and bound.

A local artist, Andrea Dopaso, was hired to watercolor about fifty original pages. "The idea of the book was to make it look like a ledger, created for the Vatican by a bookkeeper, to inventory all the Bernini work commissioned by the Pope," says Dopaso.

Using books from the sixteenth and seventeenth centuries, the artist copied the aging palette. "I scanned the pages of the old books and the watercolors and composed them in Photoshop to create each page," says Dopaso. "Almost each of them has different aging. I did the text by hand with pen and ink. I used a real Vatican ledger, from the Getty Museum, as reference. Also you can see the bleeding coming from the back of each page, to give them a feel of a real book."

The book took months and months of work. "It's just one scene in the movie," admits Trish Gallaher Glenn, "but it's a really important clue, and we don't really know how the actors are going to use it. As it turned out, the pages were shot extensively in close-up."

L'estasi di Santa Teresa

Incaricato dal
Cardinale Federico Cornaro
nel dì 6 agosto de l'anno 1645

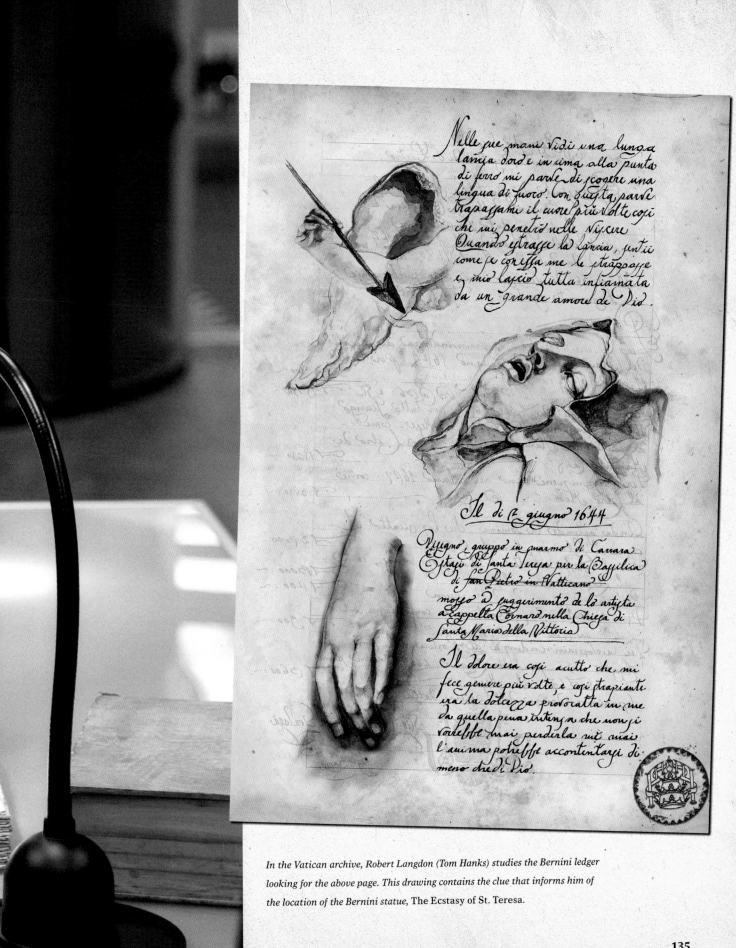

In the Vatican archive, Robert Langdon (Tom Hanks) studies the Bernini ledger looking for the above page. This drawing contains the clue that informs him of the location of the Bernini statue, The Ecstasy of St. Teresa.

...as he inspects the bookshelf.

Move over as...

SHOT	FRAME

...Langdon inspects the glass wall, then TILT down to meet Chartrand.

SHOT	FRAME

SHOT	FRAME

Chartrand POV - Fading.

SHOT	FRAME

Follow Langdon around the bookshelf.

SHOT	FRAME

...as he tests its sturdiness.

SHOT	FRAME

SHOT	FRAME

Langdon begins climbing up the shelf.

SHOT	FRAME

SHOT	FRAME

Knocking books out to the floor.

SHOT	FRAME

He looks back. Pull out -

SHOT	FRAME

... as Langdon passes his feet onto a steel girder.

SHOT	FRAME

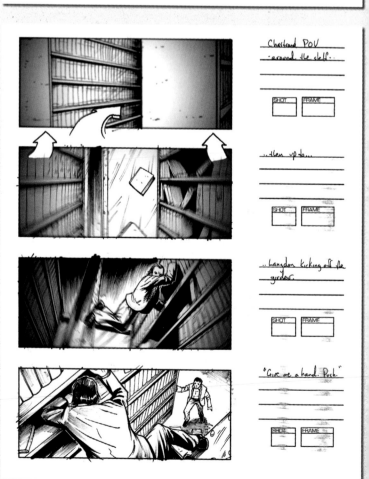

Chartrand POV around the shelf.

SHOT	FRAME

...then up to...

SHOT	FRAME

...Langdon kicking off the girder.

SHOT	FRAME

"Give me a hand. Push."

SHOT	FRAME

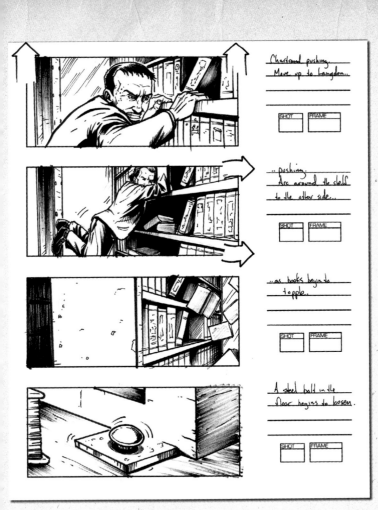

Chartrand pushing.
Move up to Langdon...

SHOT | FRAME

..pushing.
Arc around the shelf
to the other side...

SHOT | FRAME

...as books begin to
topple.

SHOT | FRAME

A steel bolt in the
floor begins to loosen.

SHOT | FRAME

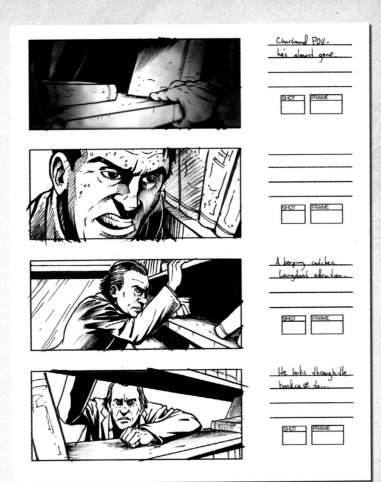

Chartrand POV -
he's almost gone.

SHOT | FRAME

SHOT | FRAME

A beeping catches
Langdon's attention...

SHOT | FRAME

He looks through the
bookcase to....

SHOT | FRAME

The oxygen level almost
depleted.

SHOT | FRAME

SHOT | FRAME

A THUMP catches
Langdon's attention -
he looks down.

SHOT | FRAME

Langdon POV - now blurring
too - on Chartrand,
now passed out.

SHOT | FRAME

Langdon strains -
pushing with every
ounce of strength.

SHOT | FRAME

Quickly BOOM up
over Langdon.

SHOT | FRAME

continue boom.

SHOT | FRAME

*Detailed storyboards visualize every shot in the scene
where Langdon escapes from the Vatican archive.
"Archive" storyboard sequence by Simeon Wilkins.*

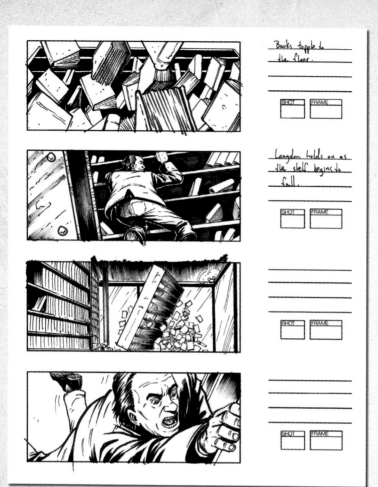

Books topple to the floor.

SHOT | FRAME

Langdon holds on as the shelf begins to fall.

SHOT | FRAME

SHOT | FRAME

SHOT | FRAME

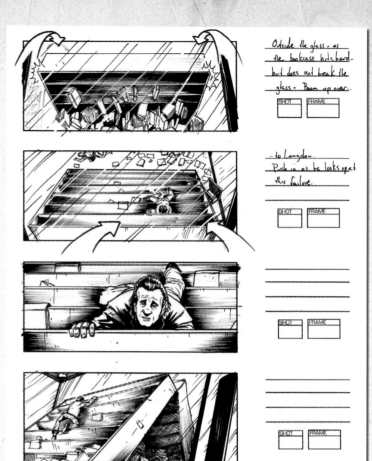

Outside the glass - as the bookcase hits hard - but does not break the glass - Boom up over.

SHOT | FRAME

..to Langdon. Push in as he looks up at this failure.

SHOT | FRAME

SHOT | FRAME

SHOT | FRAME

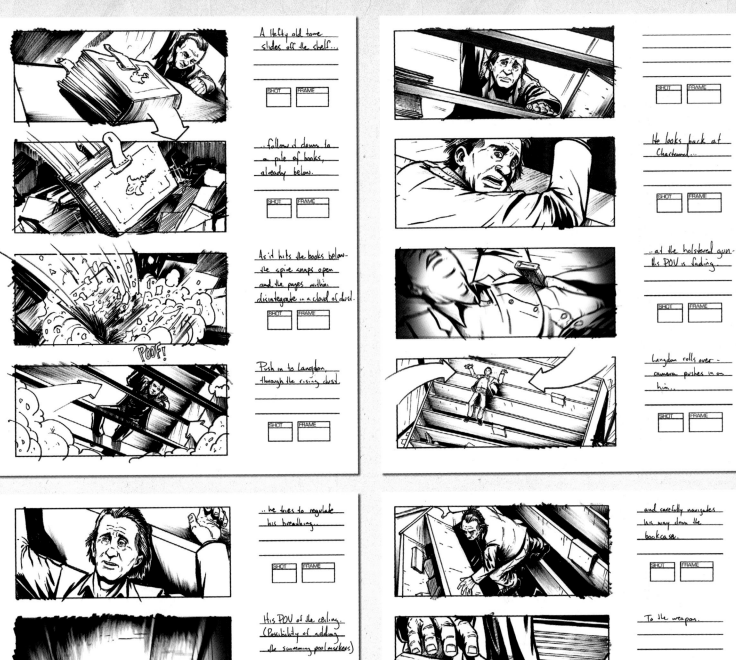

A hefty old tome
slides off the shelf...

SHOT | FRAME

...follow it down to
a pile of books,
already below.

SHOT | FRAME

As it hits the books below
the spine snaps open
and the pages within
disintegrate in a cloud of dust.

POOF!

SHOT | FRAME

Push in to Langdon,
through the rising dust

SHOT | FRAME

He looks back at
Chartrand...

SHOT | FRAME

...at the holstered gun.
His POV is fading.

SHOT | FRAME

Langdon rolls over -
camera pushes in on
him...

SHOT | FRAME

...he tries to regulate
his breathing...

SHOT | FRAME

His POV of the ceiling.
(Possibility of adding
the swimming pool markers)

SHOT | FRAME

SHOT | FRAME

Rack focus over the
gun on Langdon as he
sits up...

SHOT | FRAME

and carefully navigates
his way down the
bookcase.

SHOT | FRAME

To the weapon.

SHOT | FRAME

SHOT | FRAME

Langdon POV of the
glass wall - fading

SHOT | FRAME

The path of light is laid,

the sacred test...

THE THIRD PILLAR

Santa Maria della Vittoria

Santa Maria della Vittoria, which was dedicated in 1605, is an intimate baroque church that houses one of Bernini's most ambitious and glorious sculptures, *The Ecstasy of St. Teresa*, completed in 1646.

The statue depicts the moment described by St. Teresa in her autobiography where an angel pierced her heart with a golden shaft, causing exquisite pain and immense joy.

Both the statue and the church play a seminal role in Dan Brown's novel, *Angels & Demons*, which was first published in 2000. Ever since, the church has become a popular tourist attraction in Rome.

ABOVE: The magnificent altar at Santa Maria della Vittoria. BELOW: Floor plan for the church. BELOW LEFT: Construction for the entrance to the church. OPPOSITE: The Bernini statue The Ecstasy of St. Teresa.

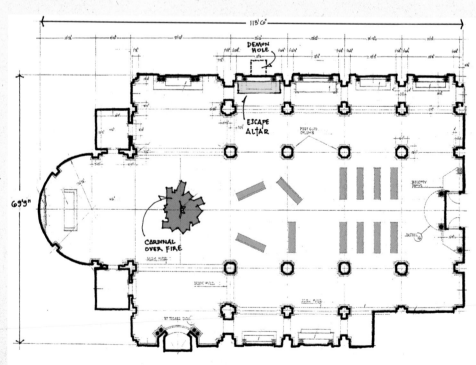

CHARTRAND:
A woman left completely afire.

The Marble Church

We tried to re-create the spirit of the real church, which is an absolutely extraordinary marble church. We spent months generating the marble wallpaper for the wall panels and floors.

The actual Santa Maria della Vittoria in Rome is quite small, and the action that takes place in the church is quite complex. Sal Totino, our director of photography, and Ron wanted to use cranes for the cameras in the church, so we had to enlarge the aisles and the nave. We made it slightly bigger than the real one in order to accommodate the action.

—Allan Cameron,
production designer

OPPOSITE: The re-created Ecstasy of St. Teresa *set piece. ABOVE: Tom Hanks on set in front of the statue. RIGHT: Detail of the altar. BELOW: The set of the church during construction. FOLLOWING PAGES: Concept drawing of the fire scene in Santa Maria della Vittoria by Allan Cameron.*

One of my favorite stops of the visitors' tour of our sets was Allan Cameron's re-creation of Santa Maria della Vittoria, especially The Ecstasy of St. Teresa. *I was not only showing off our art department's skill and talent, but I also felt like I was doing those people a favor in saving them the trip to the real church in Rome. The detail work is stunning.* —RON HOWARD, DIRECTOR

A Church on Fire

Capturing fire is very hard but, with new bits of what is called fluid dynamics software, we are starting to create good computer-generated fire. I consider our actual job to be invisible augmentation. We make the scene more dramatic by adding bigger flames, spitting embers, a heat haze, and maybe a bit more smoke.

We actually had a surprisingly big fire going for real on the set of Santa Maria della Vittoria. The flaming pile of wooden pews and chairs is actually a metal structure that comes apart and can be moved.

Clay Pinney and his special effects team laced these gas-fed flame forks and pipes through the metal structure when we were on set. This way we could establish a level that was practical on the stage.

Then we took the same sculpture out into the back lot at Hollywood Park, where Clay could go wild. We turned it up to 11 for our various shots. We spent two nights with that bonfire. Then we added some CG elements for dramatic effect.

Of course, we had a stuntman playing the Cardinal who hangs over the top of the fire. He is supported by wires, which we paint out. We genuinely got a lot of smoke and flames on the set. The trick was that Bob Yerkes, the stuntman, was actually hanging three or four feet back from the fire.

—*Angus Bickerton, visual effects supervisor*

OPPOSITE and ABOVE: In scenes shot on the Santa Maria della Vittoria set, the Cardinal is discovered hanging from the ceiling while the church below him burns.

Having done Backdraft *with Todd Hallowell and special effects supervisor Clay Pinney, we all faced the fire inside the church with real trepidation. The good news is that since our days of fire mortars and rooms that were literally ablaze, digital effects have made working with fire at least some degree safer. It's still among the most dangerous circumstances that you can work under on a film and great precautions were taken.* —RON HOWARD, DIRECTOR

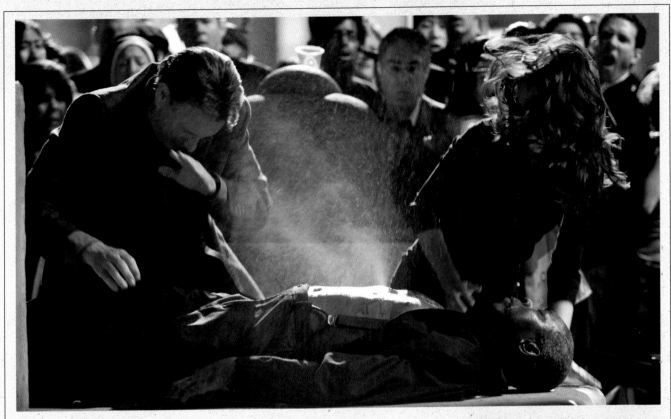

Artificial Realism

Many of the scenes in the movie required prosthetic bodies, which would be branded, burned, buried, and otherwise destroyed. All of the created prosthetics were amazingly lifelike. ABOVE: Langdon and Vetra examine the body of the "air" Cardinal. RIGHT: The real statue in the church of Santa Maria della Vittoria. This statue was re-created to melt in the fire in the church. BELOW RIGHT: The mold for the face of the statue was cast from production secretary Charlotte Rapak.

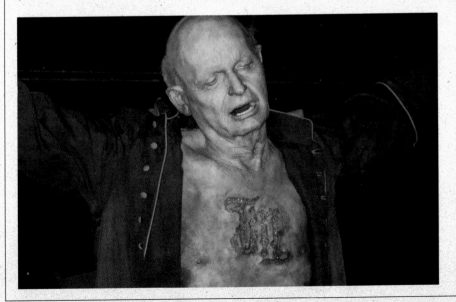

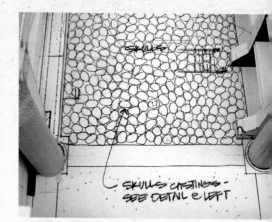

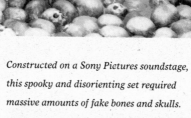

When Langdon descends into the second demon hole in the movie, he discovers a multitude of decomposed body parts and skeletons.

Constructed on a Sony Pictures soundstage, this spooky and disorienting set required massive amounts of fake bones and skulls.

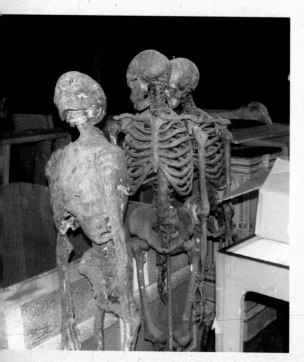

Let angels guide thee

on thy lofty quest.

THE FOURTH PILLAR

Converting St. Peter's Square

We had six weeks to convert St. Peter's Square to Piazza Navona.

First we struck the entire basilica end of our St. Peter's Square. Then we built the foundation for the Bernini statue, *Fontana dei Quattro Fiumi* (*Fountain of the Four Rivers*).

We had to dig a pond through the asphalt. We hired a swimming pool contractor and dug down 3½ feet into the tarmac to excavate a pool area. Special effects had to pipe in water and add cables for the lights and to heat the water.

One other interesting aspect of this set is that we actually shot some of the exteriors in Rome. This is when Tom Hanks drives into the piazza. He gets out of the police car in Rome, but he walks onto my set in Los Angeles. I had to make sure the two knitted together seamlessly.

—Allan Cameron,
production designer

ABOVE: Scale models of the set for Piazza Navona, which was designed to be converted from the St. Peter's Square set. BELOW: Production designer Allan Cameron on location at the Hollywood Park racetrack. OPPOSITE: The actual Fontana del Moro *in Piazza Navona.*

CALZEDONIA

OSTERIA

TRE LUPINI

GELATO

TRATTORIA ROMANA

BUILDING #7
GELATERIA

BUILDING #8
OSTERIA

BUILDING #8 cont.
OSTERIA

ELEVATION A

ELEVATION

BLOCK I

ABOVE: Concept drawing by Allan Cameron for the Piazza Navona set. OPPOSITE: Technical set plans for the buildings that surround Piazza Navona. BELOW: Piazza Navona in Rome.

The size of two football fields, the set for both St. Peter's Square and, later, Piazza Navona was started in London, completed in Los Angeles, and took about five months of work. Every detail referenced the original sites. Once the set for St. Peter's Square was struck, the filmmakers had about six weeks to convert it to Piazza Navona, a job that required digging into the tarmac to create a 3½-foot-deep pond for the Fountain of the Four Rivers. Because an important scene takes place inside the fountain, the water needed to be heated, making construction even more complicated. The photographs on these pages show the progression of converting St. Peter's Square to Piazza Navona.

Piazza Navona

Three flamboyant baroque statues in Piazza Navona make it one of the most dramatic and theatrical of all piazzas in Rome. The baroque style is also represented in the colorful buildings that surround the piazza.

Over the centuries, Piazza Navona has been a marketplace and has hosted theatrical shows and races. For two centuries, from 1650 to 1866, it was flooded (by stopping the fountain outlets) every weekend in August for elaborate celebrations.

Today the site is a popular tourist attraction with numerous cafés, shops, stalls, and street entertainers.

The entire production was giddy the day that we walked onto Piazza Navona and the achievement was made all the more clear because we had filmed at the real Piazza Navona. And what we were going to do was a cinematic meld between the real Piazza Navona and this one, which we could control at Hollywood Park. The artistry required to carve and shape and paint both locations was beyond anything I'd ever really seen. —RON HOWARD, DIRECTOR

ABOVE and RIGHT: The final dressed set for Piazza Navona.

162

The Fountain of the Four Rivers

Bernini's *Fontana dei Quattro Fiumi*, or the *Fountain of the Four Rivers*, was unveiled in 1651. At first the piece, commissioned by Pope Innocent X, was very unpopular, mainly because it was paid for by a tax levied on bread and other staples during a time of horrific famine throughout Italy. Today, of course, it is recognized as a seminal piece of baroque art and one of Bernini's masterpieces.

The fountain celebrates four rivers—the Ganges, the Danube, the Nile, and the Plate—which are symbolized by four giants.

The filmmakers wanted to shoot the actual fountain in Piazza Navona, but soon discovered that it was under restoration. "We were allowed access to Piazza Navona," explains Angus Bickerton, "but the problem was that the Four Rivers fountain was still clad in scaffolding, despite the Italians assuring us that the restoration would be finished."

Without the actual fountain, the filmmakers decided that a replica would have to be built from scratch for the very important scene with one of the four kidnapped Cardinals.

LEFT: An amazing reproduction of Bernini's masterpiece Fontana dei Quattro Fiumi *(the Fountain of the Four Rivers) was created for the Piazza Navona set. ABOVE: Director Ron Howard in front of the fountain.*

ABOVE: The art department's photo reference board for the sculptures. Many of the maquettes (clay models) are seen in various states of progress. LEFT: Preliminary maquettes for the Fountain of the Four Rivers. RIGHT: The maquette in the foreground of the photo shows the scale relationship between the clay model and the full-sized sculpture in its raw foam state. BELOW: The finished forms are painted to add color and texture. OPPOSITE: The finished Ganges figure in the studio (left) and on the set.

Making Monuments

For *Angels & Demons*, sculptor foreman Martin Smeaton was asked to create twenty freestanding sculptures and many smaller items such as plaques and reliefs. Having worked with production designer Allan Cameron on *The Da Vinci Code* (among many other films, operas, and plays), Smeaton began his work, as always, by studying reference books, photographs, and art department drawings of the sets. Scaled maquettes were then made for all the individual sculptures.

"Photographs of these models were imported into computer programs such as Photoshop to help with realization of size in relationship to the rest of the set," explains Smeaton. "For single large sculptures, the final medium is usually high-density expanded foam. Smaller items are sculpted in the traditional way with water-based clay. Molds are made and then cast in either plaster or fiberglass. There inevitably comes a time when it depends on the skill of the sculptor to complete the sculpture. On the large foam pieces, the finish is achieved by a lot of fine sanding, arriving finally at a polished gesso finish which looks remarkably like marble even before it's painted."

While the sculptures are meant to represent the original works of art, Smeaton admits that making an exact replica is impossible and not always desirable. "It depends on the work, but for the most part I think the integrity of the set is what's most important," says Smeaton.

"Sometimes you need to simplify an overcomplicated piece of sculpture. Trying to understand what the camera sees can change things dramatically. Also, the dimensions of the set can change and the sculpture has to change proportionately."

Smeaton's sculpture department consisted of eight artists working in both London and L.A. Each of the four statues in the *Fountain of the Four Rivers* took about five weeks to complete.

Interestingly, there were times during the creative process that Smeaton realized he shared the same challenges as Bernini himself. "On a purely physical level, we sometimes come across the same problems in the work that the original artist must've experienced and it surprises me that the same solutions remain just as valid today," says Smeaton.

"When working on a piece you realize that perhaps the hair looks familiar, then you discover its similarity to a Michelangelo sculpture. Obviously, Bernini looked at the works of past sculptors for inspiration to solve his problem. This trail of creativity runs down through the centuries."

Smeaton points out another important similarity between his work and Bernini's: "Often after completing a project you want to distance yourself. After finishing *Angels & Demons*, I didn't want to look at Bernini again for a while. Then I learned that after the *Fountain of the Four Rivers* was completed, Bernini would pass through Piazza Navona in his carriage and draw the curtain so he wouldn't have to see the structure and be reminded of all the things he should have done."

Shooting in the Fountain of the Four Rivers

LEFT: Ron Howard discussing storyboards for an upcoming scene. ABOVE: The fountains at night. OPPOSITE ABOVE: The cast and water safety crew members working on the scene that takes place inside the fountain. RIGHT: The cast and crew preparing to shoot the complicated scene.

BELOW: Marco Fiorini plays Cardinal Baggia, one of the four kidnapped Cardinals, who has the "water" ambigram branded on his chest. The actor was strapped into a harness and lowered into the fountain for this climactic scene.

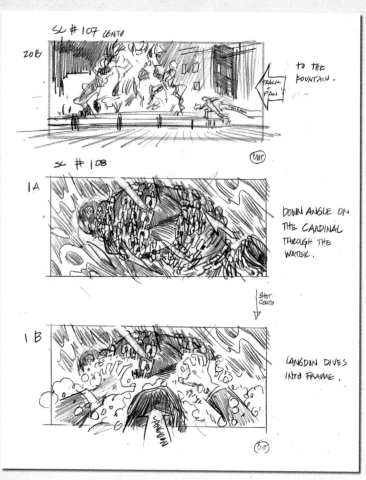

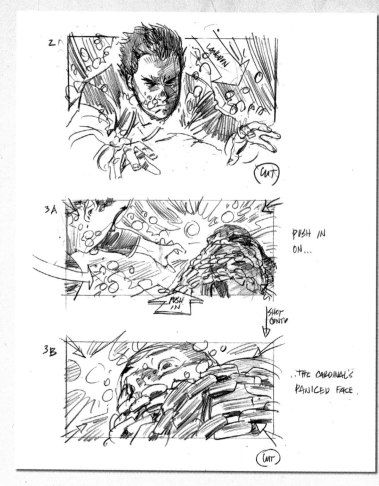

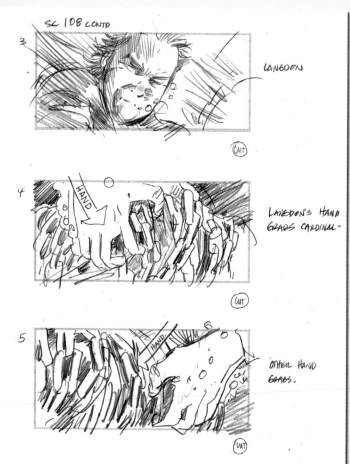

SC #107 CONT'D

20B

to the
FOUNTAIN.

CUT

SC #108

1A

DOWN ANGLE ON
THE CARDINAL
THROUGH THE
WATER.

SHOT
CONT'D

1B

LANGDON DIVES
INTO FRAME.

CUT

2

CUT

3A

PUSH IN
ON...

PUSH
IN

SHOT
CONT'D

3B

...THE CARDINAL'S
PANICED FACE

CUT

SC 108 CONT'D

3

LANGDON

CUT

4

HAND

LANGDON'S HAND
GRABS CARDINAL-

CUT

5

HAND

OTHER HAND
GRABS.

CUT

SCENE # 108 CONT'D

6A

TILT
UP

SHOT
CONT'D

6B

PUSH UP TO
LANGDON'S
FACE -

BOOM
UP

SHOT
CONT'D

6C

AS HE STRAINS
TO LIFT.

BOOM
UP

CUT

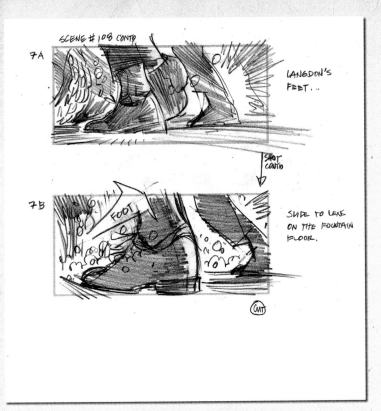

7A — SCENE #108 CONT'D — LANGDON'S FEET...

7B — SLIDE TO LEAN ON THE FOUNTAIN FLOOR.

Storyboards of the scene where Langdon dives into the Fountain of the Four Rivers to save one of the kidnapped Cardinals. "Water" sequence storyboards by Gabriel Hardman.

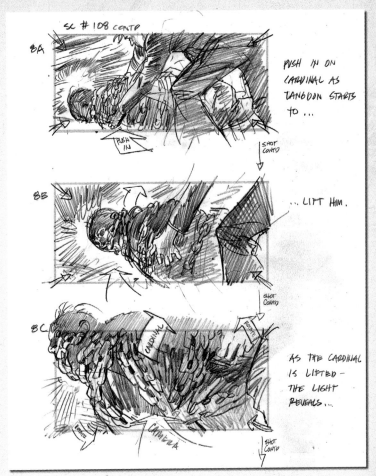

SC #108 CONT'D

8A — PUSH IN ON CARDINAL AS LANGDON STARTS TO...

8B — ...LIFT HIM.

8C — AS THE CARDINAL IS LIFTED — THE LIGHT REVEALS...

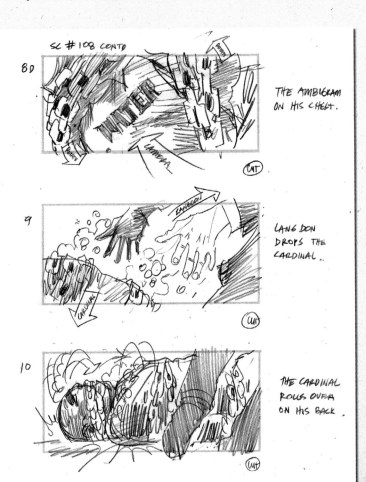

SC #108 CONT'D

8D — THE AMBIGRAM ON HIS CHEST.

9 — LANGDON DROPS THE CARDINAL...

10 — THE CARDINAL ROLLS OVER ON HIS BACK.

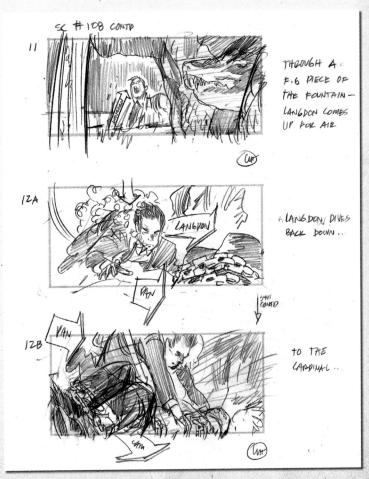

SC #108 CONT'D

11 — THROUGH A F.G PIECE OF THE FOUNTAIN — LANGDON COMES UP FOR AIR

12A — LANGDON DIVES BACK DOWN...

12B — TO THE CARDINAL...

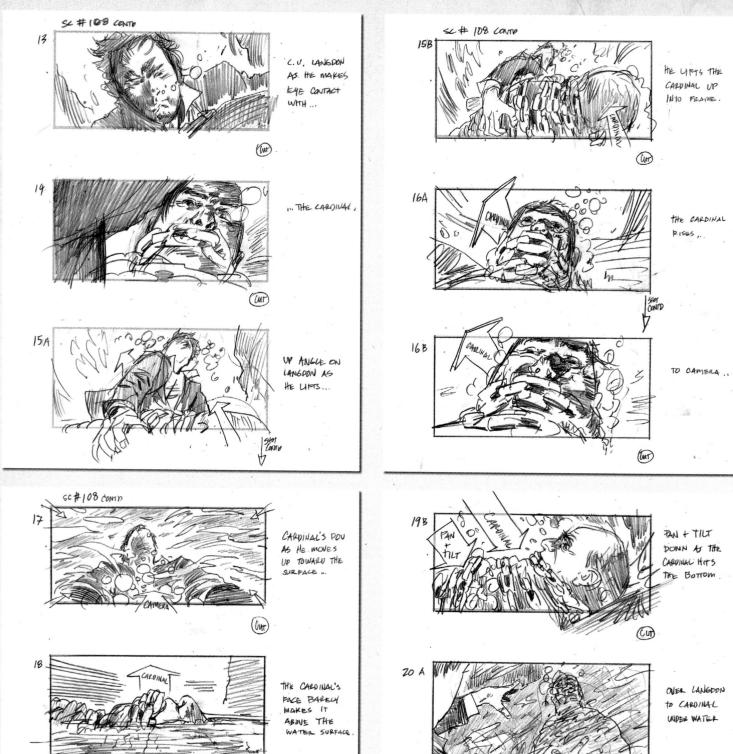

SC #108 CONTD

13   C.U. LANGDON
      AS HE MAKES
      EYE CONTACT
      WITH...
      CUT

14   ...THE CARDINAL,
      CUT

15A   UP ANGLE ON
      LANGDON AS
      HE LIFTS...
      SHOT CONTD

SC # 108 CONTD

15B   HE LIFTS THE
      CARDINAL UP
      INTO FRAME.
      CUT

16A   THE CARDINAL
      RISES...
      SHOT CONTD

16B   TO CAMERA..
      CUT

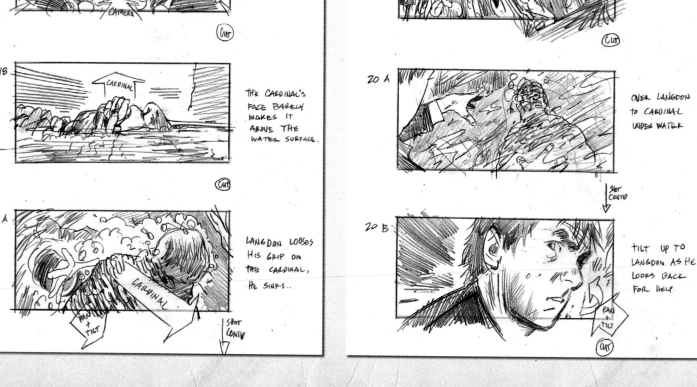

SC #108 CONTD

17   CARDINAL'S POV
      AS HE MOVES
      UP TOWARD THE
      SURFACE..
      CAMERA
      CUT

18   THE CARDINAL'S
      FACE BARELY
      MAKES IT
      ABOVE THE
      WATER SURFACE.
      CARDINAL
      CUT

19A   LANGDON LOOSES
      HIS GRIP ON
      THE CARDINAL,
      HE SINKS..
      CARDINAL
      PAN + TILT
      SHOT CONTD

19B   PAN + TILT
      DOWN AS THE
      CARDINAL HITS
      THE BOTTOM
      PAN + TILT
      CARDINAL
      CUT

20A   OVER LANGDON
      TO CARDINAL
      UNDER WATER
      SHOT CONTD

20B   TILT UP TO
      LANGDON AS HE
      LOOKS BACK
      FOR HELP.
      PAN + TILT
      CUT

SC # 108 CONTD

21
OVER LANGDON.
A STREET
SWEEPER BETWEEN
HIM AND THE
PEOPLE AT THE
CAFE.

22A
LONG LENS
ON STREET
SWEEPER...

22B
...AS IT
EXITS. REVEALING
LANGDON. HE
YELLS FOR HELP.

SC # 108 CONTD

23
THE STREET
CLEANER STOPS
IN FRONT OF
THE CAFE.

24A
LANGDON...

24B
...TURNS. LOOKING
FOR SOMETHING
THAT WILL HELP
HIM.

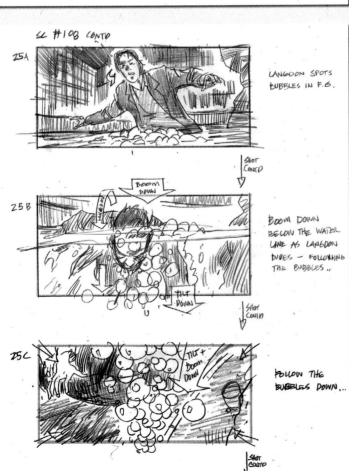

SC #108 CONTD

25A
LANGDON SPOTS
BUBBLES IN F.G.

25B
BOOM DOWN
BELOW THE WATER
LINE AS LANGDON
DIVES - FOLLOWING
THE BUBBLES...

25C
FOLLOW THE
BUBBLES DOWN...

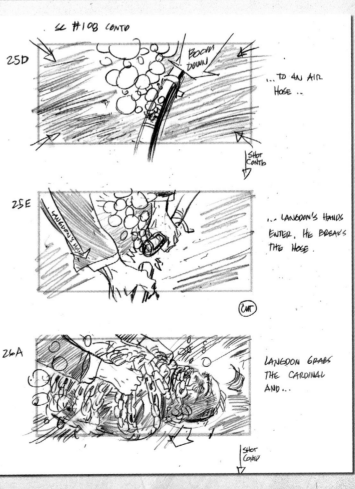

SC #108 CONTD

25D
...TO AN AIR
HOSE...

25E
...LANGDON'S HANDS
ENTER. HE BREAKS
THE HOSE.

26A
LANGDON GRABS
THE CARDINAL
AND...

A Shining Star at

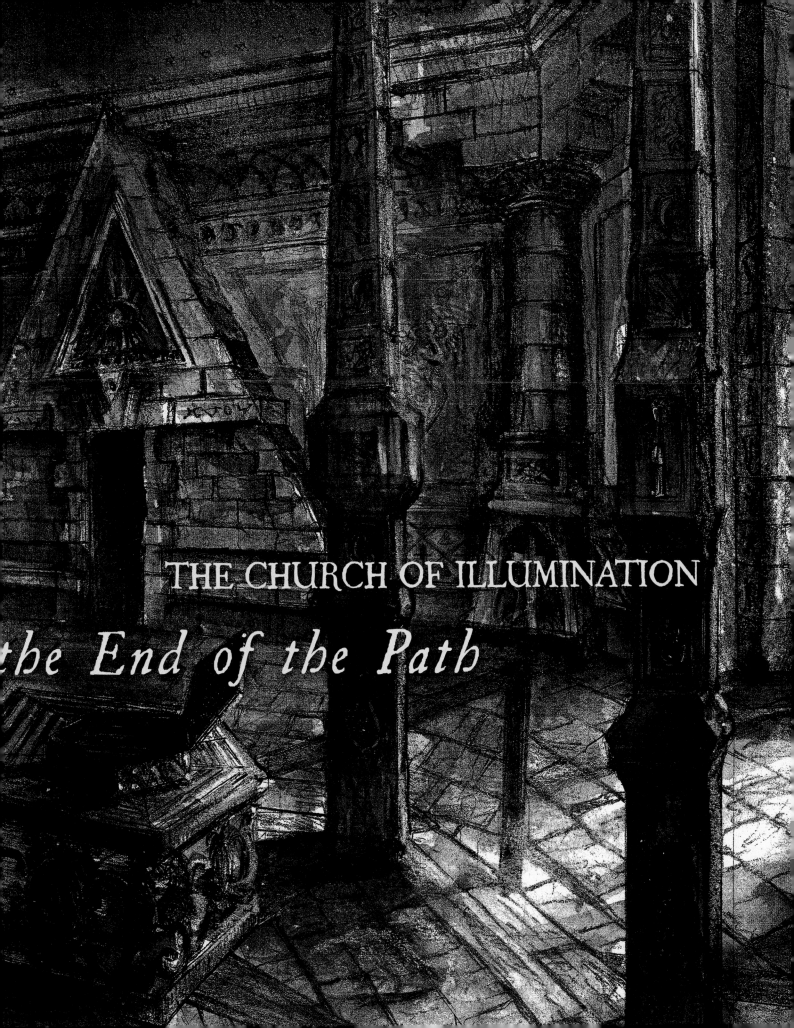

THE CHURCH OF ILLUMINATION

the End of the Path

Interior of the Church of Illumination

Castel Sant'Angelo

Castel Sant'Angelo is a massive fortress that was originally created as a mausoleum for Emperor Hadrian in A.D. 139. Since then it has played many roles as a medieval citadel and prison, as well as home to many Popes during times of political trouble. Today it is a 58-room museum that details all aspects of the castle's history.

For *Angels & Demons*, the location represents the end game where the chase to find the antimatter canister comes to a fiery conclusion. A great deal of action happens here, including a wild chase through the underground tombs.

PREVIOUS SPREAD and ABOVE: Concept drawings of the Castel Sant'Angelo by Allan Cameron. LEFT: Set decoration detail. RIGHT: Hanks on location at the Castel Sant'Angelo.

Langdon and Vittoria creep into the Church of Illumination. The embellishments, though faded, are replete with familiar symbology. Pentagram tiles. Planet frescoes. Pyramids.

LEFT: The Il Passetto set was the only scene shot on the European streets on the Universal lot. ABOVE: Robert Langdon and Vittoria Vetra run across the Il Passetto. RIGHT: Prison cells inside the Castel Sant'Angelo where the Cardinals were held captive.

LEFT and ABOVE: Concept drawings of the cells by Allan Cameron.

BELOW: Nikolaj Kaas plays Mr. Gray, the assassin.

ABOVE: Early concept sketch for the Necropolis set. TOP: Concept drawing by Allan Cameron. ABOVE RIGHT and RIGHT: Scale models of the Necropolis pathways. LEFT: Early rendition of the antimatter canister. FAR RIGHT: Robert Langdon, Vittoria Vetra, Chartrand, and the Camerlengo discover the hidden antimatter canister.

UNDERGROUND

There's a small stone chamber, part of an archeological dig in progress. The Camerlengo moves more tarps and construction materials inside, revealing a soft glow emanating from underground.

We come over his shoulder and see what he sees: a small, hollowed-out area in which a work light, taped to a battery pack, serves as a light source for a video camera on a small tripod. And in front of the camera's lens—

is the glowing canister of antimatter.

The Helicopter

THIS PAGE: *The helicopter was used twice in the movie, once as a Vatican aircraft and, in the finale, as a medi-vac. The actual helicopter purchased for the film could not fly and all the dials on the control panel were purchased separately.* OPPOSITE: *The scene for the final explosion was shot with a green screen background and then computer enhanced in post-production.*

The Antimatter Explosion

The explosion near the end of the film was where we strayed from the known, realistic world; this is a bit of fantasy in which a tiny particle, less than a gram, of antimatter leads to a cataclysmic explosion in the sky. I think the script says it is the equivalent of 10 kilotons.

We had no precedent for creating this explosion, so we had to make certain leaps of imagination. My concern was to make this feel believable. We looked at reference footage of real nuclear explosions and tried to build a look that taps into things we already know.

We are not necessarily creating a mushroom cloud; nuclear explosions in the air look completely different from the ones on the ground. Those explosions kick off the ground, which creates that famous mushroom shape. In the atmosphere with no confinement, it becomes almost like a doughnut ring; the pressure of the atmosphere holds it in one layer.

The Americans and the Russians continue to test the biggest bombs they can, short of nuclear, so we have been looking at the atmospheric effects of the blast and shock waves. I have looked at the terrible things that happen when rockets explode during launch, huge fuel payloads. We've been tapping into and referencing all those to build the look.

—*Angus Bickerton, visual effects supervisor*

Concept art for the final climactic explosion.

SCENE # 180

1A

WIDE. BASILICA
TRACK LEFT AS
CAMERLENGO
ENTERS THROUGH
A DOOR...

TRACK

SHOT
CONT'D

1B

..HE HEADS
TOWARD LENS...

TRACK

SHOT
CONT'D

1C

PAN
BACK

CAMERLENGO

TRACK

TRACK + PAN
BACK W/ HIM
AS HE HEADS...

SHOT
CONT'D

SC. # 180 CONT'D

1D

PAN

CAMERLENGO

DOOR
OPENING

CUT

TOWARD THE MAIN
ENTRANCE. HE
STOPS

2

REACTS.

CUT

3

HIS CHEATED P.O.V.
HALF A DOZEN SWISS
GUARD BLOCK HIS
PATH.

CUT

SC # 180 CONT'D

4A
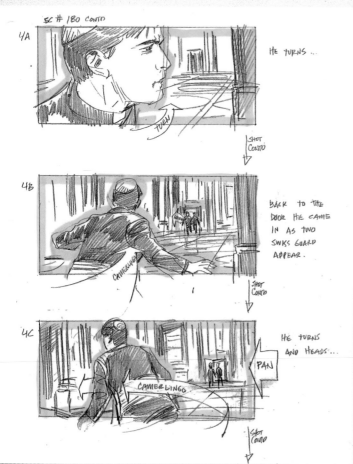

TURN

HE TURNS..

SHOT
CONT'D

4B

CAMERLENGO

BACK TO THE
DOOR HE CAME
IN AS TWO
SWISS GUARD
APPEAR.

SHOT
CONT'D

4C

CAMERLINGO

PAN

HE TURNS
AND HEADS...

SHOT
CONT'D

SC # 180 CONT'D

4D
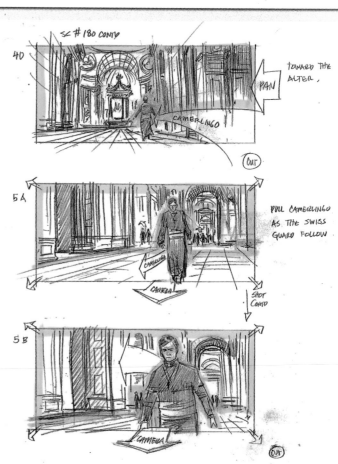

PAN

CAMERLINGO

CUT

TOWARD THE
ALTER.

5A

CAMERLINGO

CAMERA

PULL CAMERLINGO
AS THE SWISS
GUARD FOLLOW

SHOT
CONT'D

5B

CAMERA

CUT

6A
ENTER
CAMERA
SHOT CONT'D

6B
HE HEADS TOWARD THE STAIRCASE...
CAMERLENGO
CAMERA
CUT

7
HIGH WIDE, PAST THE HIGH ALTER. HE HEADS TOWARD THE STAIRCASE.
BOOM DOWN
CUT

SC # 180 CONT'D

8
UP STAIRS AS CAMERLENGO ENTERS AND LOOKS DOWN.
CUT

9
HIS POV OF THE LAMP HE BROKE EARLIER.
CUT

10A
CAMERLENGO LOOKS UP. PAN TO:
PAN
SHOT CONT'D

10B
PAN
A FRESH LAMP AS HE GRABS IT.
CUT

Storyboards detail the sequence where the Camerlengo commits a dramatic, fiery suicide. (The highlighted areas represent green-screened sections of the set.) "Immolation" sequence storyboards by Gabriel Hardman.

SC # 180 CONT'D

11
FOLLOW GUARD. THEY HEAR A CRY AND LIQUID SLOSHING.
CAMERA
CUT

12
THE GUARD REACT THEN RUN OUT OF FRAME.
EXIT
CUT

13
THEIR POV, PUSH TOWARD THE STAIRS.
BOOM DOWN
CAMERA
CUT

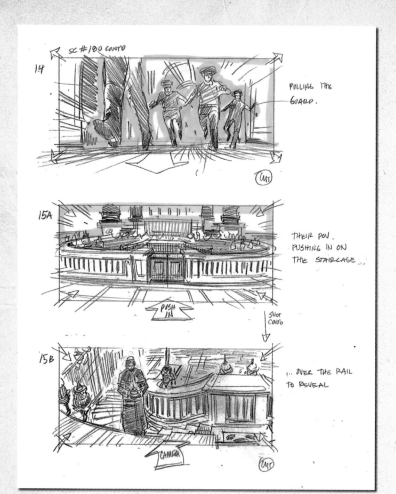

SC #180 CONT'D

14 — PULLING THE GUARD.

15A — THEIR POV. PUSHING IN ON THE STAIRCASE...

PUSH IN

SHOT CONT'D

15B — ...OVER THE RAIL TO REVEAL

CAMERA

17A — LOW PAST THE LAMP TO

SHOT CONT'D

17B — HE DROPS THE LAMP.

LAMP

18 — THE LAMP SMASHES AT HIS FEE

LAMP

19A — WIDE THE FLAMES ENGULF HIM.

19B — HE DROPS TO HIS KNEES — STILL STOIC.

20A — BOOM UP. DOWN ANGLE ON HIM. BOOM UP AS THE FLAMES CLIMB..

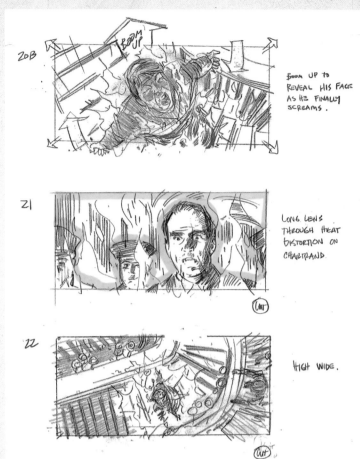

20B — BOOM UP. BOOM UP TO REVEAL HIS FACE AS HE FINALLY SCREAMS.

21 — LONG LENS THROUGH HEAT DISTORTION ON CHARTRAND.

22 — HIGH WIDE.

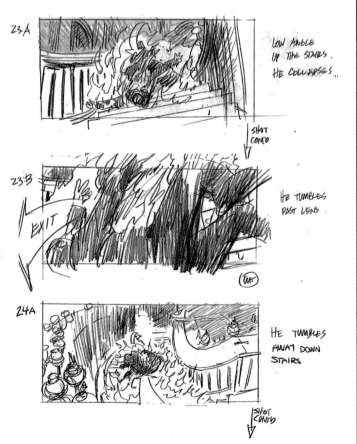

23A — LOW ANGLE UP THE STAIRS. HE COLLAPSES..

23B — EXIT. HE TUMBLES PAST LENS.

24A — HE TUMBLES AWAY DOWN STAIRS.

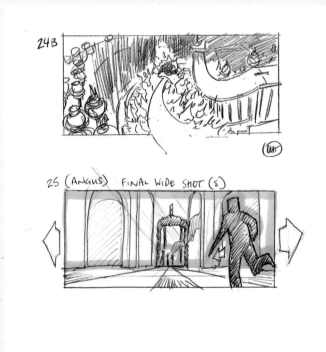

24B

25 (ANGUS) FINAL WIDE SHOT (S)

VITTORIA: He chose the name Luke.

LANGDON: There have been many Marks and Johns, never a Luke.

STRAUSS: It's said he was a doctor.

VITTORIA: That's quite a message. Science and faith all in one.